Competability

A Practical Guide to Building a Peaceable Kingdom Between Cats and Dogs

By

AMY D. SHOJAI

THREE RIVERS PRESS / NEW YORK

Although a strong proponent of pet responsibility, the author recognizes that some owners choose not to benefit from neutering their pets, and that some pets are allowed to roam. While these are facts of life for many dogs and cats, such lifestyles can present unique and difficult obstacles to building a peaceable kingdom. Hopefully this book will change many pet lives for the better. Please understand that when reference is made to such situations, the author is acknowledging the realities of—but in no way condoning—such owner choices.

In addition, the author has made every effort to provide the most current information regarding pets and their care; however, the understanding of veterinary medicine, pet behavior, and training is constantly improving. Provide optimum health care for your pets by regularly consulting a veterinarian. Ongoing behavior problems are best addressed by a professional pet therapist, behaviorist, or trainer.

Published by Three Rivers Press, a division of Crown Publishers, Inc.,
201 East 50th Street, New York, NY 10022

Random House, Inc. New York, Toronto, London, Sydney, Auckland.
www.randomhouse.com/

THREE RIVERS PRESS and colophon are trademarks
of Crown Publishers, Inc.

Design by June Bennett-Tantillo

Printed in the United States of America

Library of Congress Cataloging in Publication Data
Shojai, Amy
Competability : a practical guide to building a peaceable kingdom
between cats and dogs / by Amy D. Shojai.—1st ed.
Includes bibliographical references and index.
1. Dogs. 2. Cats. I. Title.
SF427.S555   1998   97-35942
636.7'0887—dc21   CIP

ISBN 0-609-80088-4

10 9 8 7 6 5 4 3 2 1

First Edition

In memory of Toby,
and all pets like him.

Dedicated to owners who strive
to do the right thing—
especially Mahmoud.

Contents

PART III: Bright-Eyed and Bushy-Tailed

PART IV: Canine Culture and Feline Language

APPENDIXES

Com*pet*ability

Introduction

❦

I've always had a passion for pets. My childhood home was bordered by open fields on two sides, a pine grove outside the front door, and a river just beyond the backyard. Visits to Grandma Monteith's lake cottage and to Grandma Stirsman's small farm helped make my childhood rich in animal adventures. Orphan bunnies and baby birds fallen from nests always found their way into my pockets. My favorite playmates were the turtles, toads, frogs and snakes, squirrels and raccoons, mice and lizards, ponies, cows, and chickens I encountered in my ramblings.

But my deepest affection was for dogs and cats.

Our family's first pet was a handsome wolf look-alike named Toby. He arrived when I was about three years old, and I loved him dearly. Although wonderfully affectionate with our family, Toby was incredibly protective of his turf, and so strong and willful that he was difficult to control. We didn't understand him, and he didn't understand us. I'm sure Toby thought he was doing his job when he guarded our yard from trespassing cats.

I was seven years old when Toby got loose for the umpteenth time and chased—but this time killed—our neighbors' cat. When I came home from school the next day, Toby was gone. Mom and Dad said he'd found a new home. It wasn't until years later that I realized what going to the animal shelter really meant.

Toby broke my heart. The big black dog didn't know any better, and our family didn't know how to help Toby learn. Even then I knew it wasn't fair. It's all too common, when things go wrong, for the pet to pay the ultimate price.

As I grew older, our family had other dogs, but never a cat—after all, dogs hate cats. Yet I knew in my soul there must be a way for the two loves of my life to live together in harmony.

Fortunately, I was right. Dogs and cats can and do live together in the same households. The ancient enmity between these species is a myth, one sadly perpetuated by unfortunate experiences such as Toby's. Since then I've done my best to educate pet owners so that the price for misunderstandings will not be paid in a pet's blood.

Over the years I've learned not only what questions to ask but where to look for answers. My experience as a veterinary technician opened my eyes to the many misconceptions concerning dogs and cats. Fifteen years ago I began addressing these issues by writing books and articles aimed at educating pet lovers about how best to care for their companion animals.

I am delighted to live in an age in which the popularity of pets is at an all-time high, and dogs and cats are being recognized for their ancient and ongoing contributions to the human experience. Surveys estimate that in the United States, Australia, France, Belgium, and Ireland, nearly 40 percent of all homes keep a dog, with slightly fewer keeping cats. There are nearly 90 million pet dogs in Western Europe and the United States, and about 95 million pet cats in the same geographic region. Some 66.2 million cats and 58 million dogs are kept by Americans.

Dogs and cats have been good to me, and I hope my writing has been good to pets. But until now there's been little opportunity for me to address an issue close to my heart.

Most of the writing on dogs and cats that deals with medical issues, care, training, and behavior (including my own writing) focuses on each species separately. This is true for the simple reason that cat articles are published in cat magazines, dog topics appear in canine publications, and pet books are typically targeted to fanciers of one species or the other. Even magazines and books that cover several different types of pets tend to keep their articles segregated, with cats in one section and dogs in another. Consequently, misconceptions about these popular pets persist.

Though they have much in common, their very differences make cats more appealing to some people than dogs, and vice versa. Dog people passionately argue in support of the obedient nature and loyalty of the canine. Those of the feline persuasion treasure the cat's style, independence, and loving individuality. And when dog lovers read only information about dogs, and cat lovers educate themselves only about cats, it's unavoidable that myths about the two become entrenched. Dog people *know* that cats can't be trained; and cat people are *convinced* that dogs blindly do whatever they're told. Both notions are wrong.

In fact, the truly enlightened among us—more than 15 million American households—double our pleasure by welcoming both dogs and cats into our homes and witness firsthand how the differences between these unique creatures complement each other. Dogs and cats each bring their own special joys to the human heart and home.

Although a mountain of information is available about cats *or* dogs, there is little guidance for pet owners who live with both. Yet mixing the two can mean trouble in paradise if you treat Kitty like Fido, or vice versa.

I broke new ground in pet publishing with an innovative topic for the annual February 1996 puppy issue of *Dog World* magazine. My article, "Living in a Peaceable Kingdom," offered basic information about introducing a new puppy to resident pets, including cats. It was a unique opportunity to discuss the relationship between these two pets in a venue targeted specifically toward a canine audience.

In the article I explained that pet owners need to familiarize themselves with a large body of information if they are to properly care for both species in the same house. Owners don't always realize that a wagging tail has opposite meanings for cats and dogs. And those who love these pets with equal passion may inadvertently put a pet's health or even life at risk. When I was still working as a vet tech, a woman fed her cat the pain medicine prescribed for her dog—aspirin—and was surprised when Kitty nearly died.

Cats and dogs are two very different animals with distinctive needs. They cannot—and must not—be treated the same way. Their structure, the way their bodies work, what they eat, how they behave, and what they want out of life are very different.

Competability explains all the ins and outs of living with and caring for cats and dogs in the same household. It shows how cats and dogs are alike and how they're different, and it offers commonsense suggestions along the way for smoothing interspecies relationships. It is the first book to put America's favorite pets on an equal footing, and address both species in a whisker-to-whisker comparison.

Com*pet*ability goes further than many how-to books that offer paint-by-number, step-by-step instructions. Pets aren't that simple, and neither are people. Instead, this book helps you *think* like your pets, so that you'll better understand them and your role in their lives. Only by knowing *why* something works are we empowered to make positive, educated choices for ourselves and our pets. Com*pet*ability will provide you with all the necessary tools to build your own peaceable kingdom with your dogs and cats.

Much of what our pets are has been influenced by human intervention—in particular, the domestication process. We have accepted these once-wild creatures into our hearts and homes, changed their destiny, and in many cases altered their function and form. As a result, the vast majority of modern pets have lost the ability to care for themselves. Pet cats and dogs are dependent upon us for shelter, food, and their life purpose. How can we complain about pet idiosyncrasies when we have played a major role in creating them?

The article in *Dog World* brought me full circle back to the little girl who still mourns Toby. I didn't know enough thirty years ago to help him, but perhaps today I can make a difference for other cats and dogs so that they can live together in harmony. And it is my fondest wish that this book will enable other fur-fanatics like me to fulfill their own pet dreams.

So as you read this, take a moment to give all your furry wonders a pat for me. And tell them Toby says hi.

PART ONE

The Common Denominator

CHAPTER ONE

❧

In the Beginning . . .

In prehistoric times people honored and revered all living things, for they understood that humans were but one part of a whole. An unspoken, unwritten covenant was made between people and the furred, feathered, and finned children of the earth—to remember and respect their common beginnings and to keep the memory sacred.

Dogs and cats are our reminder of that ancient covenant. They reflect some of the best features of the human soul, offering us childlike honesty, unreserved devotion, and a love that has no parallel in human experience.

More than any other creature, cats and dogs have been accepted, even welcomed, into the human family. It's remarkable that such very different creatures should hold the same intimate relationship with people. These special companion animals continue to honor their beginnings, and it is our responsibility to honor them by becoming sensitive to their needs.

To understand the similarities and the differences between modern dogs and cats, we must look to their earliest beginnings. In fact, cats and dogs arose from a common ancestor. The story begins about 220 million years ago when mammals first arrived on the prehistoric scene.

CREODONTS AND MIACIDS

The Jurassic and Cretaceous periods were host to countless predatory reptiles and dinosaurs, large and small, that ate one

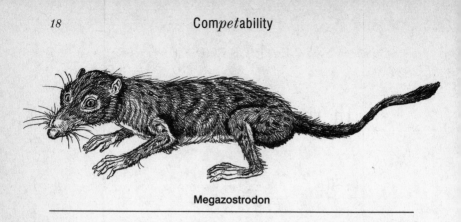

Megazostrodon

another as well as the mammals that were just appearing. Massive carnosaurs, or "flesh lizards," like the tyrannosaurs dominated life during the Jurassic and Cretaceous periods.

Two new kinds of predators called creodonts and miacids evolved from early insect-eating mammals like Megazostrodon. These early flesh-eating mammals emerged about 65 million years ago; however, they were outclassed and outhunted by the already established meat-eating dinosaurs of the day. Consequently, the evolutionary growth of creodonts and miacids remained at a standstill for some time.

Then a miracle of sorts happened. At the end of the Mesozoic Era, about 65 million years ago, dinosaurs ceased to exist. A general consensus is growing within the scientific community that an asteroid hit caused such a worldwide catastrophe that none of the larger lifeforms survived. The mass die-off gave mammals the opportunity they needed. Their differences from the other creatures apparently better equipped them not only to survive the mysterious event but to thrive as well.

Suddenly the world was devoid of large predators. Without natural enemies, the hairy plant-eating mammals grew bigger and slower, multiplying into vast slow-moving herds that spread through much of the ancient world. Onetime prey animals were no longer hunted, and they lost their fear of attack.

Creodonts and miacids moved into the ecological niche left empty by the death of the predatory dinosaurs. Both creatures began to evolve into a variety of new forms better able to profit from the host of easy prey. Creodonts flourished and became the predominant flesh-eating mammals throughout the world, remaining so for nearly 9 million years.

Creodonts developed in a variety of ways and mirrored many forms of modern-day meat eaters. Just as the predators changed with the times, so did their prey. The slow-moving herds of plant eaters learned to fear the meat-eating creodonts and began to evolve in ways that would enable them to protect themselves. Grazing animals became smarter, grew long tusks and horns to protect themselves, and became fast enough to outrun their attackers.

The highly successful creodonts never evolved to compensate for these new developments, and we don't know why they didn't. Perhaps limited intelligence, coupled with lack of further development, resulted in the disappearance of creodonts by the Late Miocene Era, about 7 million years ago.

THE ASCENT OF CARNIVORES

Meanwhile, the lowly miacids had been quietly scampering through the forests, waiting in the wings for just such an opportunity as the creodonts' demise offered. Although creodonts were meat eaters, miacids were the earliest true carnivores to appear in the world. The word "carnivore" means animal-eater, but the term is further defined by the presence of specialized meat-shearing molars called carnassial teeth. Miacids were the first to possess these innovative choppers.

Though smaller in size, early miacids may have resembled the creodonts in some ways, but they had larger brains and were likely much more intelligent. They also had greater agility and were probably equally at home scuttling through undergrowth or leaping among the branches of trees. Some had retractable claws similar to those of modern cats.

About 35 million years ago during the Oligocene Era, miacids underwent a burst of evolution which created a wide array of creatures that replaced creodonts as the dominant predator. The miacid is considered the common ancestor of all

Miacis

modern carnivores, from fin-footed meat eaters like seals and walruses to split-footed predators with toes, like the weasel and bear. And the miacid is the many times great-grandfather of both cats and dogs.

CATS AND DOGS DIVERGE

Two catlike families, the nimravids and the felids, began to appear in the Early Oligocene Era, about 35 million years ago. They probably competed with early dogs for the same prey, or even preyed upon one another. Nimravids were the earliest cats to evolve. They had longer bodies and shorter legs than modern felines. *Nimravus* may have looked similar to the modern caracal of Africa, and had partially retractable claws. However, this family of cat is not related to modern felines; nimravids died out about 8 million years ago.

The felids outlived the nimravids and became the ancestors of all modern cats. Two distinct forms evolved within this family, reflecting their style of killing prey. These were the biting cats and the saber-toothed cats. Biting cats broke the victim's neck with their long canine teeth, as do most modern small cats, including the domestic kitty sitting in your lap. Saber-toothed cats used huge stabbing canine teeth to deeply wound their prey; then they simply waited for the animal to bleed to death.

Dog- and cat-creatures were already developing their own styles of hunting, and the changes in their bodies reflected these needs. Meat eaters in the wild never got a free lunch but had to work hard to capture prey that was mobile and intent on surviving and protecting itself. While the grazing vegetarian's diet was literally there for the picking, the carnivore's food fought back. Food animals were evolving as fast as their predators, each creature's advances pressing changes in the other.

There were two methods of bringing food to the figurative table: by chasing it down or ambushing it. The structure of modern cats and dogs reflects their preferred technique, but ancient cat and dog forms probably used combinations of both.

Some early dogs didn't look much like today's dogs. One of the earliest was a small, long-bodied, short-legged creature called the *Hesperocyon*. This little guy appeared during the Late Eocene Era, approximately 40 million years ago. He was about 2½ feet long and probably looked more like a mongoose than a modern canine. The *Phlaocyon* arose about 25 million years ago and resembled a raccoon; other dog ancestors looked and probably acted more like hyenas and scavenged food leavings from other carnivores.

The *Cynodesmus,* one of the first creatures to actually resemble a modern dog, appeared about the same time as the *Phlaocyon.* He probably looked like today's coyote but had a much blunter nose. The *Cynodesmus* walked on his toes like modern dogs, but had partially retractable claws and probably ambushed small prey in the style of a fox or a cat.

In addition to the saber-toothed cats and the smaller-fanged biting cats, false saber-toothed cats had large stabbing canines sized midway between the two. Some were called dirk-toothed cats because their teeth resembled daggers, while others with backward-curving bladelike teeth were described as scimitar-toothed cats. A typical false saber-tooth was the *Eusmilus,* a large leopard-size cat that first appeared in Europe about 40 million years ago.

Big-toothed cats like the *Smilodon* preyed on the large, slow-moving mammoth and bison. The jaws of the *Smilodon* were designed to open more than 120 degrees to allow the huge saber-like teeth to penetrate the thick skin of the prey. The *Smilodon* probably lived in large social groups like modern lions, and fossil evidence suggests he could both roar and purr.

The dog family continued to evolve as well. The *Osteoborus* was a hyenalike dog that appeared about 8 million years ago. He probably lived in packs that scavenged the remains of food after other predators had finished, or simply stole the prize away from inattentive owners.

About 5 million years ago, the land bridge between North America and South America appeared, and canids finally began the trek out of their homeland. One of these creatures, the *Cerdocyon,* was an early fox. He lives on in the modern crab-eating zorro of Colombia and Argentina.

Canids took the place of other predators when they became extinct and competed with felids for the same prey. When the *Osteoborus* disappeared about 2 million years ago, *Canis dirus,* the dire wolf, was there to take his place. This large prehistoric wolf was a heavier version of the modern wolf. But evidence suggests the dire wolf was more scavenger than hunter and may have been a camp follower of the saber-toothed cat, *Smilodon.*

In fact, saber-tooths and dire wolves engaged in ferocious battles over food, but neither of these prehistoric animals was smart enough to avoid following prey animals into sticky tar pits. The sight of a giant sloth or elephant thrashing helplessly about in the tar must have been too much of a temptation to resist. Excavations of the La Brea tar pits in Los Angeles revealed the remains of more than two thousand dire wolves and *Smilodons* trapped alongside their prey.

About 2 million years ago, at the end of the Pleistocene Era, many mammalian species including mammoths and woolly rhinoceroses died out during the last great Ice Age. These creatures had also been extensively hunted by early humans. With the large prey animals gone, prehistoric felids and canids—and people—had to find something else to eat.

Dire wolf

Those who couldn't adapt to the fleeter prey that remained didn't survive. Dire wolves and saber-toothed cats became extinct, making way for smarter, more adaptable hunters.

MODERN RACES

The differences between the wildcats and wolves that replaced prehistoric critters grew more distinct. The dogs developed into endurance specialists who used their slashing teeth and powerful jaws to capture and hold prey. The cats became stalkers who relied on stealth, speed, stabbing teeth, and specialized retractable claws to grapple prey.

Felids developed into the two feline divisions we recognize today. Those referred to as *Panthera* include the big cats: lions, tigers, panthers, and jaguars. All the smaller cats, including the one that's currently teasing your dog, are referred to as *Felis*. Canids diversified into fox, jackal, coyote, wild dogs (like Cape hunting dogs and dingoes), domestic dogs, and wolves.

The skeletal structure between these related but distinct animals remains uniquely canine or feline. Nearly all felids (except the cheetah, which runs down its prey, like a dog) rely on stalking and pouncing abilities, and nearly all canids (except the fox, which stalks and pounces like a cat) run down their prey. The most obvious differences within the cat and dog races are in size. Where the game was larger, the cat and dog species grew bigger to prey on antelope, zebra, and elk. Smaller felines and canines hunted smaller animals like rabbits, squirrels, and mice.

The social structure of both types of animals is directly related to the size of the prey. Smaller carnivores like bobcats and foxes usually hunt alone and feed on small prey that an individual is able to kill. Because most of these small cat species come together rarely, perhaps only during breeding seasons, there isn't a need for highly developed social behavior.

Larger carnivores such as wolves and lions have a much more highly developed social system. In order to survive, they require far greater quantities of food. Big prey fit the bill, but are often difficult for a solitary predator to bring down. For that reason, lions, cheetahs, and wolves became social hunters that depend upon the cooperation of the group to bring down larger prey.

THE ADAPTABLE CAT

Although there was some behavioral and social crossover between the wildcat and wolf races, most cats survived primarily as solitary animals that hunted alone. Females raised their young without help from the males. It's a feature of cats that the young mature and become independent very early in life. Because group living was not important, there was no need for a sophisticated pecking order to keep the peace. Instead, cats more often interacted one-on-one in sexual and territorial matters, and in these cases simply determining which of the two is the top cat was sufficient.

Cat paws developed almost handlike dexterity, with razor-sharp retractable claws used for clinging to struggling prey or as grappling hooks to scramble up trees. Most cats stalked or ambushed their swift prey, then killed with a bite to the back of the neck. And cats, particularly the smaller varieties, preferred night-stalking. Consequently, their eyes evolved to better capture and make use of low light, and their hearing became fine-tuned to detect the most subtle rustle or squeak. Cats haunted the grassy fields and scrubby woods and forests, which provided them with the cover they needed to stalk their favorite foods.

But cats painted themselves into a corner by relying so heavily on meat. Though they relished eating the vegetable contents of a victim's stomach, cats became obligate carnivores that needed to eat meat, and lots of it, to survive.

CANINE CONTRASTS

Wolves evolved into social creatures that hunted and lived in family groups or packs. Members of the group, both males and females, helped feed, protect, and rear the young. Since communal life required optimal communication among pack members, dogs developed sophisticated body language and vocalizations. A hierarchy evolved as well in which dominant animals ruled subordinates, a survival mechanism that reflected their need to get along well together with a minimum of disputes.

Physically, wolf claws became heavier, blunter, and more protective. Paws became less able to grasp, and the wolf muzzle lengthened to better hold and capture prey. The toe-walking (digitigrade) canine foot was well suited to hunting swift antelope on the open grasslands, but it was equally adaptable to open woods, and the resulting longer stride provided swiftness and stamina that enabled the wolf to run down speedy animals.

Relying on intelligence as well as brawn, wolves used teamwork to chase prey animals and run them to exhaustion. Instead of the lethal neck bite used by cats, they slashed and tore the victim until it became weakened from blood loss—similar, in fact, to the saber-toothed cats of yore.

Their senses sharpened, particularly scenting ability, which helped canids identify friend, foe, and food over long distances. And just as importantly, they became omnivores. Canids preferred a meat diet, but became physically able to survive as vegetarians if the necessity arose. This was most likely an inherited mechanism; when meat was scarce, canids not able to switch gears to a vegetarian diet didn't survive to pass on this trait to offspring, while those with more flexible tastes did.

THE HUMAN PREDATOR

It is probable, even likely, that early man had an ongoing relationship with wildcats and wolves. The earliest humans preyed primarily on the woolly mammoth and rhinoceros; as long as this food was plentiful, they may not have been in direct competition with the cat and dog races. Wildcats and wolves probably weren't terribly important to early humans until the extinction of the large, slow-moving food animals. Then, just like the cat- and dog-creatures, people were forced to hunt alternative prey, and the three became rivals.

Early people probably considered wolves and wildcats a nuisance at best and a danger at worst. After all, furry predators were taking food off the human table. Humans probably hunted and ate dogs and cats from time to time, and certainly wore their fur. In a one-on-one confrontation, the hairless, comparatively fragile human would probably have lost the battle and ended up an appetizer in a kitty or doggy dinner.

But the animals as well as the humans couldn't have helped but notice the advantages of an interactive relationship. Humans must have admired the stealth and hunting prowess of cats, and the incredible scenting ability of dogs, who found prey that was invisible to humans—wolves could identify weaker animals and cut them out of the herd.

How did cats and dogs make that final leap away from the forest and fields and into the human ring of firelight? While the answer remains shrouded in mystery, archaeological evidence supports a number of theories. Canine and feline bones found adjacent to ancient human settlements have placed dog domestication at about 15,000 years ago and cat domestication nearly 5,000 years ago. But because it can be difficult to tell a wild dog or cat skeleton from that of a domesticated animal, even the experts argue about dates, and no definitive answer has been determined. Furthermore, recent genetic analysis of fossil remains indicates that dogs may have been domesticated 100,000 years ago, much earlier than the archaeological record indicates.

The domestication process didn't happen overnight. In fact, it is likely that wolves and wildcats domesticated themselves to a great extent. Although the canine potential caught human attention much earlier than cats did, in the end both creatures became equally beloved.

CHAPTER TWO

❧

A Match Made in Heaven

Domestication has affected cats and dogs in both subtle and obvious ways. The very term "domesticate" means to alter or change a once-wild creature to one that can live harmoniously with people and for their benefit. But from which wild creatures did our dogs and cats descend—and when?

The mostly likely ancestral forebear of domestic cats is the African wildcat, or Kaffir cat *(Felis silvestris libyca)*. Although larger than domestic varieties, he prefers to live near humans and is easily tamed, unlike some other wildcat contenders. Even more telling, he is able to breed successfully with domestic cats.

It is generally agreed that the cat was first domesticated by the Egyptians about 3000 B.C. All modern domestic cats, including nearly fifty distinct breeds and countless random-bred variations, are designated *Felis catus*.

The definitive ancestral dog is much more difficult to pinpoint because modern dogs are so much further removed from their wild roots. Most experts hold that modern dogs have in their heritage one or more species of wolf from interbreeding at different times in their history. The small eastern Asiatic wolf *(Canis lupus arabs)* is thought to have heavily influenced most European and southern Asiatic dogs, including the dingo. The small Chinese wolf *(Canis lupus chanco)* probably gave rise to Chinese dogs while the North American wolf was the most probable founding canine father of Eskimo dogs. More than four hundred distinct canine breeds are recognized around the world. All domestic dogs, including purebreds and random-bred combinations, are designated *Canis familiaris*.

Whatever the genetic soup, dogs and cats are far removed from their wild ancestors, in great part because of humans. To see the dramatic influence that domestication has had on these animals, simply compare a wolf to a Chihuahua or a Saint Bernard, or compare a wildcat to a Persian.

Even more telling, the psychological and emotional makeup of the wolf and that of the wildcat have been transformed. Although some behavior patterns are innate, domestication has rendered most pet dogs and cats unsuited for life on the wild side. There may be an ancestral wolf or wildcat buried deep beneath the fur, but dogs and cats are no longer wild animals. Today's pets live with people because they must; they can't survive on their own.

THE TIE THAT BINDS

Why would early humans want to domesticate a wolf or a wildcat? Remember, people considered these animals competitors. They might have admired their hunting prowess, but surely they feared the animals' aggressiveness. It's likely that every human social group routinely lost members to a ferocious wolf or cat-creature. The bravest, most celebrated members of the tribe were those who survived such attacks and even overcame these creatures and lived to wear trophies of pelts, fangs, or claws. The first person to say, "He followed me home, can I keep him?" must have been greeted with jeers at best.

Early humans began to domesticate animals when they recognized a potential benefit, and the dog was the first creature to be domesticated. Some of the earliest evidence of this canine-human association was found at an excavation site in northern Israel that dates from 12,000 years ago. It revealed a human skeleton alongside that of a puppy, with the person's hand placed across the puppy's chest as though with affection.

It's likely that scavenging was the first tie binding dogs and people. As early humans hunted, slaughtered, and feasted upon available prey, the leftovers must have been an irresistible lure to scavenging wolves. Some wolf families became experts at the snatch-and-grab, waiting in the bushes until the time was right, then sneaking close to grab a mouthful of deer meat.

Consequently, some wolves abandoned hunting for the easy pickings of these garbage dumps. Packs followed human hunters or made their homes near human settlements. And instead of chasing them away, early people welcomed these wolf beggars, and even encouraged them to stay.

What benefit did wolves bring to the campsite? Canine families living near people would have been a desirable addition to a human community because of their territorial nature. The bark or howl that alerted other wolves to danger also gave warning to humans, and the watchdog—er, watchwolf—was born.

The domestication process was not a one-sided affair, however. It's hard to imagine that people woke up one day and consciously decided to tame a wolf and create a new creature. It's much more likely that domestication was accidental and that wolves entered the process as willing participants. Instinct for survival would have caused early wolves to select the safest and most productive manner of securing food and shelter. A relationship with people offered that and more.

For a time, wolf families would have coexisted alongside their human counterparts. Wolf packs and human society became a familiar part of life for each other, though they lived apart. But just as many modern children and adults are fond of baby animals, it's possible that prehistoric humans, delighted by wolf cubs, adopted the young of camp-following packs as pets.

Furthermore, the hierarchical social structure of wolves closely paralleled that of humans. Baby wolves raised with people fit right in, transferring their allegiance to the human pack with whom they lived. And as human youngsters grew up alongside the wolf cubs, the affection between the two must have grown strong. Unlike other wild animals, wolf cubs that are handled and played with don't outgrow their fondness and respect for people, but retain tame behavior as adults.

Over time, generations of these wolves lived with people and the most responsive of them were bred, so that the qualities people found desirable in the selected parent wolves would be inherited by their offspring. A strain of tame wolves was probably established very quickly.

Both early people and wolves were highly intelligent predators who roamed vast territories seeking similar prey. The hunting and social behavior of both evolved as a direct result of the harsh Ice Age environment, where group hunting of large mammals was a necessity for survival.

About 10,000 years ago during the Mesolithic Period, human hunters seem to have recognized another benefit of the relationship. Using their extraordinary observational skills, wolves were able to pick out prey, separate it from the others, then herd it toward waiting pack members. People harnessed this talent for themselves by selecting the best herders from among their tame wolves. This teamwork, innate to wolf packs, was simply modified to include humans.

What did each species get out of the relationship? When game was scarce, combining forces offered both parties a better chance of success. Instead of competing, everybody won. People were no longer left in the dust chasing a herd animal they had no hope of catching. Wolves found the prey and chased it, but didn't need to attempt a kill, risking injury or death from sharp hooves or horns. Most likely the wolf was rewarded for a successful hunt with prime selections from the kill.

Over time, these camp wolves changed as a result of their relationship to humans as well as the conditions of the time. During the Pleistocene Period, about 14,000 years ago, the harsh conditions of the Ice Age began to change. The earth warmed, climate improved, and the size of many of the existing mammals grew smaller.

Once a very large animal, the wolf eventually decreased in size. The long, narrow muzzle, so important to capturing prey, shortened as killing food was no longer its central means of survival. This foreshortening of the muzzle caused a crowding of the teeth rows and a reduction in tooth size.

At the same time, human societies of the Mesolithic Period started gathering wild grain in addition to hunting game, and they eventually traded the restless life for more permanent settlements. And the short-distance hunting style of rushing with stone ax and club evolved into longer-distance hunting with spear and arrow. It's believed that this change in human hunting technique spurred the wolf-human partnership as tame wolves followed people throughout the world, tracking game, pointing it out, and retrieving it after it was killed.

Physical changes like the foreshortened muzzle and smaller size made it more difficult for the tame wolf to live successfully in the wild. These short-faced wolves were the precursors of true dogs, and took the first tentative steps over the threshold into domestication.

LIFE IN THE SHADOWS

While humans and wolves recognized a mutual advantage to developing a relationship, wildcats remained on the fringes, avoiding contact with humans. After all, cats were quite successful as solitary hunters, and an association with humans offered them few benefits. Early man's admiration for cats is evidenced by cave drawings of lions and other prehistoric feline art. But it's doubtful that humans and wildcats sought out each other's company, unless it was to hunt each other.

Feline philosophy and social structure were as foreign to early man as the wolves' pack mentality was familiar. The cat was a mystery to be pondered, to be revered, but not to be understood, and certainly not exploited. The cat's hunting prowess was much respected, but unlike the wolf, it was not so easily harnessed.

The early human hunting societies offered little to attract wildcats, either. Although not above stealing another cat's kill, felines tend not to be scavengers; they prefer fresh prey. The proximity of wolves probably kept smaller cats at bay, removing them farther from close contact with humans. Furthermore, wolves were already a successful hunting tool, and they were much more easily utilized than the unpredictable cat. Thus, for the first 8,000 or so years of doggy domestication, cats clung to their wild ways and walked their own separate path.

FROM WOLF TO WHELP

It's impossible to pinpoint exactly when wolves evolved into dogs. Archaeological evidence based on the relationship of the animals' location to human habitation, as well as the shortened jaws and smaller teeth of early dogs, has led some experts to theorize that the first truly domesticated dogs appeared in Mesopotamia and, from there, spread through Asia and into Europe. The earliest domesticated dogs in North America were found in Jaguar Cave, Idaho, and date from about 10,000 years ago.

Early on, humans saw many potential benefits to keeping dogs. They served as watchdogs and guards, got rid of disease-producing garbage by scavenging the remains, slept with humans as furry bed-warmers, found and retrieved prey, or herded animals to slaughter. And dogs could themselves be eaten when game was scarce. The ecosystems of ancient Mexico, for instance, had no large game animals, and the Aztecs ate wild turkeys and ducks, along with an assortment of dogs bred specifically for the table.

But not all dogs were bred for utilitarian purposes. The Aztecs also kept Chihuahua-type dogs specifically as pets. And about 5,500 years ago, the Chinese were breeding tiny "sleeve dogs," cherished pets that their owners carried wherever they went.

Three basic early dog types arose, each influenced by the environment and man's selective breeding. Probably the first modern canines to appear were the polar, or spitz-type, dogs that accompanied the early nomads who hunted within the Arctic Circle and that may have looked similar to today's Alaskan Malamute.

The pariah dog developed in southern Asia and northern Africa, while the dingo made his way to Australia with the help of seafaring people. These ancient medium-size dogs with curled tails are still found in their native lands today. The climate demanded short fur, and their coats probably came in a variety of colors.

The third ancient type was probably bred from pariah-dingo stock by selecting dogs with great speed and good vision. Called gazehounds or sight hounds, these canines relied on vision rather than smell during the hunt and were ideally suited to hot desert climates, which offered high visibility but made scenting difficult. Sight hounds have been bred in the Middle East for at least 6,000 years—the Upper Egyptian culture circa 4240 B.C. worshiped Set, a dog with a forked tail that looks very similar to the modern Greyhound—and modern dogs like the Borzoi, Afghan Hound, and Whippet look very similar to these ancient breeds. In fact, the Saluki of Asia Minor is probably the oldest dog breed still in existence.

Dogs became valuable members of the emerging agricultural societies. They were trained to herd livestock, protect it from predators, and even serve as a kind of movable fence by keeping cattle, goats, and sheep from eating the fields of grain.

INTO THE LIGHT

It is commonly accepted that cats were first domesticated in ancient Egypt. It is doubtful that the domestication of cats was planned; as with wolves, it simply happened when the time was right.

The earliest evidence to support true domestication dates from about 1600 B.C. A combination of factors probably influenced feline domestication, the most pressing being a change in the social and economic environments. Prior to 7000 B.C., wildcats competed with people for birds and other small game as a food supply. But when the hunter-gatherer societies were transformed into agricultural communities of cultivators and herders, and the early settlement economy became largely grain-based, the role and behavioral patterns changed.

Simply put, hanging out near people became profitable for the cat. The large centralized supply of food animals like goats, sheep, and cattle surrounding human settlements drew the large cat predators, including lions and leopards. Furthermore, grain stores attracted vermin, which in turn provided a ready food supply that the wildcats relished.

At first, the presence of cats was probably a mixed blessing for people. After all, along with that lamb or kid, the lion also occasionally carried off a human shepherd. But hand-reared cheetahs proved to be nearly doglike in obedience and became popular as coursers of antelope alongside Greyhounds. And people clearly saw the advantages of using cats to patrol granaries. Most likely, the natural selection process encouraged the rise of tamer wildcats that were more tolerant of living alongside humans on farms and in villages. People and wildcats probably lived side by side from about 7000 to 4000 B.C. Savvy humans began setting out food offerings to keep the half-wild felines nearby, and the wildcats subsisted on a combination of handouts and vermin.

During this 3,000-year span, Egyptian culture was obsessed with animals of all kinds, not just dogs and cats, and common people as well as nobles and kings all tamed and kept animals as pets. Those animals that adapted more easily to a life with humans would have been mated with others similarly well socialized, and their offspring in turn were even more docile and amenable to a tame existence. Consequently, a unique coexistence among species developed in which wildcats and Pharaoh Hound–type dogs served alongside each other to protect the grain from rodents, and tamed cheetahs and sight hounds were used to course larger game. Paintings found in Theban tombs dating from about 1450 B.C. indicate that hunters may have preferred wildcats for marsh hunting and employed them as flushers and retrievers of birds.

Religions arose that honored cats and mythological feline creatures. As early as 3000 B.C., pictures, icons, statues, and amulets featuring cats were an everyday part of Egyptian culture. The religious and cultural life of ancient Mesopotamia so revered the feline mystique that eventually the cat was glorified as a god, outshining even the lion, leopard, bull, and wolf-dog deities of the day.

The popularity of the cat reached its zenith about 950 B.C., in Bubastis, an Egyptian city on the Nile Delta. The society worshiped a cat-headed goddess called Bast, or Pasht, and domestic cats were seen as incarnations of the goddess on earth.

By this time domestic dogs were established nearly everywhere in the world where humans were found, but cats were jealously guarded treasures and were not allowed to leave Egypt. Some cats, however, were inevitably stolen and smuggled out of the country.

From Egypt, the domestic cat traveled first to Persia, China, Japan, and Greece. But most regions preferred other animals for rodent patrol, and domestic cats remained a rare curiosity throughout much of the world for some time.

From the Mediterranean, cats traveled throughout the Roman Empire and beyond. They seem to have been established in Italy by A.D. 400, in Switzerland by A.D. 200, and in Britain by A.D. 400. They made their way to Germany 600 years later. By the tenth century, cats were widespread, though still uncommon, throughout most of Europe and Asia.

DOGGED EXAMPLES

From the prototypical dog and cat arose an array of canine and feline forms, some by accident and others by human design. Canine mutations that served a purpose were encouraged.

One of the first mutations in both dogs and cats was coat type. No longer requiring wild camouflage, domestic dogs sported a wide variety of coat types, ranging from smooth to shaggy and from solid colors to brindle (having dark streaks) or even spotted. The mummified remains of ancient Egyptian dogs sport the tan coat color common to the modern wild pariah dogs of India and dingoes of Australia, which are descendants of some of the earliest domesticated canines. Some historians speculate that this mutation in color not only differentiated between the wild wolves and the domestic dogs but that the gene which influenced coat color also affected the dog's temperament. This mutation was encouraged because tan dogs were often tamer.

Some of these mutations would have died out through natural selection if canines had lived in the wild state; instead, they were protected and even promoted through the process of domestication. As a result, features such as coat type and color, body shape and size, length of the muzzle, and placement of the ears began to change, resulting in the wide range of dog breeds seen today.

Each innovation served a distinct purpose. Long, rough coats made some dogs more resistant to harsh, cold climates. Small dogs were valued for their ability to control vermin while big ones could protect livestock. Short-legged dogs could follow their prey into varmint holes, while long-nosed, pendulous-eared dogs were better sniffers. Local populations of prehistoric dogs began to look different from one another as early as 5000 B.C. And by 1000 B.C., the main lines of dogs we recognize today were well established and served specific needs.

The Arctic, or spitz, breeds were used in a number of ways. Dogs like the Samoyed herded reindeer and pulled sleds, while in China the Chow Chow was a hunter, guardian, and sled dog. These dogs developed heavy double coats to protect them in cold climates.

Other mutations were related to size. Giantism (acromegaly) was promoted in certain dogs, and created new breeds. The giant Mastiffs, with their massive bones and muscles and their exaggerated facial features, were used as war dogs, guardians, and hunters of the largest game. Other giant dogs that fulfilled the same roles included wolfhounds and boarhounds. Modern examples include the Great Dane, Saint Bernard, and Newfoundland.

The earliest members of the hound group, including the Greyhound and Saluki, evolved to hunt the open plains using their sharp eyesight. They swiftly ran down prey, but quickly lost interest in the chase if the quarry ran out of sight.

By the time of the Greeks, a variety of scent hounds were being developed. These dogs were slow but sure hunters whose stamina was designed to wear down prey. Modern examples are the Foxhound and the Beagle.

Belowground hounds that "went to earth," following badgers and foxes into their dens, were also bred. Dwarfism (achondroplasia) was promoted to create specialized breeds. As dwarfism caused curved, foreshortened limbs, leaving the body and head relatively proportional, short-legged dogs similar to the modern Basset Hound and Dachshund were ideal for hunting in the narrow burrows of badgers and other animals. The most ancient dwarf dog is the Pekingese, bred in China for at least 3,000 years, which served as a companion. Miniature dogs like the modern Italian Greyhound and a variety of tiny terriers were smaller than but otherwise proportionally nearly identical to full-size animals; they hunted rats and other underground vermin.

*CAT*EGORIES

Domestication had very little impact on the physical evolution of cats. After all, feline service to people remained similar to what cats had always done—hunt, kill, and eat small prey. But once Kitty began traveling, local environments and normal inbreeding did generate differences. While humans had been molding dogs into a variety of sizes and shapes for literally centuries, nature stepped in to promote certain characteristics that made cats in certain regions different from those anywhere else.

Geneticists refer to the *seven ancient mutations,* which are thought to have occurred quite early in feline domestication. The cold climates of the Chorazan province (a mountainous region) in ancient Persia (now Iran and Turkey) and the southwestern areas of the former Soviet Union probably account in part for one of the first mutations, as cats began to be born with long fur. The longhaired Persian and Turkish Angora breeds evolved in the high elevations of these regions.

The vertical stripes of the mackerel tabby, found also in the African wildcat, offered camouflage for cats living in the open grasslands. It's speculated that cats living on the fringes of forests and jungles first developed the classic tabby coat pattern. The swirls and bull's-eye patterns better concealed them in this environment.

The solid, or self-colored, cat is yet another mutation, with solid black cats being the most common. And yet another mutation is the gene for solid white cats. Under natural conditions, white cats would have been at an extreme disadvantage in the wild. They probably wouldn't have survived for long without human intervention, particularly since this gene combination can also result in deafness.

The sex-linked orange-red color occurs most frequently in Southeast Asia and Japan. The mutation may have arisen first in these regions and later spread throughout the world. Examples include calico cats (white with patches of red and black), tortoiseshell cats (black with red mingled through the coat), and torbie cats (tabby with patches of red). These color combinations usually appear only in female cats because of the genetic material required to carry these colors. Male cats with these colors are rare, and when they do occur the cat is usually sterile. The sixth and seventh color mutations are the white spotting factor and the dilution system that turns black to gray and red to cream.

But aside from coat length and color differences, cats continued to look very similar the world over. Two basic cat types eventually evolved: the cold-climate body was short, square, and compact, with a broad head, small ears, a short muzzle, round eyes, and a thick weather-resistant double coat; these cats appeared in the colder climates of Europe. Today's British Shorthair and the Persian are two examples of what's referred to in professional circles as the cobby cat type.

The warm-weather body type is a lithe and muscular cat with long, lean legs, a whiplike tail, large ears, slanting eyes, a long muzzle, a narrow wedge-shaped face, and a thin silky single coat. These cats developed in the more temperate climates of Asia. Today's Siamese cat is the prototypical Oriental type.

Cats appear to have been quite uncommon in northern Europe, even after being introduced there about the tenth century. Though cats remained quite rare in England, they were highly prized as mousers and ratters. The popularity of cats increased when Crusaders returning from the Middle East accidentally carried hitchhiking rats with them aboard their ships. Other seafarers also took cats along to help control pests, and the fame of the cat spread the world over, eventually arriving in North America with early English colonists.

TRYING TIMES

The Middle Ages in Europe were a time of conflict and change for people as well as the animals that lived with them. Both dogs and cats were persecuted during this period, and they lost much ground in their relationship with people.

As Christianity spread, displacing earlier religions, the church adopted pagan celebrations and symbols for its own purposes. Because of her dedication to her offspring, the cat was initially equated with the Virgin Mary. The highly symbolic art of the day reinforced this positive view, representing the cat as good and the mouse and rat as evil.

Yet with the increase in religious fanaticism over the centuries, the cats' connection to early pagan religions (after all, the cat had been worshiped as a god in ancient Egypt) placed them irrevocably on the wrong side of the fence. The church found a convenient scapegoat in the cat. Regarded as handmaidens of

Satan and the familiars of witches, even seen as the devil himself, cats were routinely rounded up, tortured, and slaughtered
as a way to eradicate the evil that humans perceived to be walking among them. Consequently there were few cats to prey upon
the plague-carrying rats that the Crusaders' ships brought back
from the Middle East. This unfortunate development facilitated
the spread of the Black Death.

During the Middle Ages, countless dogs were abandoned
throughout the world as their owners traveled to fight foreign
wars. Packs of stray dogs roamed cities and farming communities, returning to the ways of their ancestors to scavenge wherever and whatever they could to survive.

Witnessing firsthand packs of wild dogs digging up graves
and feasting upon the newly buried, the uneducated masses readily believed apocryphal tales of despicable doglike creatures such
as werewolves. The church had a terrible opinion of dogs, calling them salacious creatures with poisonous bites (rabies), and
priests were forbidden to keep them. In fact, the words "dog"
and "cur" were common curses.

Yet once the attention was focused upon ridding the world
of the evil feline, dogs regained their status as faithful servants,
and it was, ironically, the vilification of the cat that saved the dog.
It became a popular pastime to breed specialized hunting dogs,
which were pampered and prized. By the Renaissance, dogs were
not only celebrated as hunters but were considered faithful companions and friends.

The Renaissance saw an explosion of wealth and prosperity
across class boundaries, which had a favorable impact on dogs.
From kings to farmers, laborers to nobles—everyone kept dogs.

Hunting dogs were exclusive to the upper classes; they ate
with their masters, sometimes from the same plate, and slept in
their beds. Some were even allowed to accompany their owners
into church.

In addition to hunting, all kinds of dog-related sports flourished, from bullbaiting to ratting. Dogs worked as herders, shepherds, even circus performers. Tiny spit dogs ran treadmills to
turn skewered meat while it cooked. By the eighteenth century,
pampered lapdogs, tiny furry versions of larger breeds, had

become popular, particularly with the ladies. The first formal dog show that compared the animals' working capabilities was staged by John Ward, an English huntsman, about 1775.

When commoners were finally allowed to hunt (although they didn't have horses), a number of specialized dog breeds developed to hunt with horsemen died out. The advent of guns prompted the breeding of new specialized gun dogs that not only searched out prey, but pointed it out, flushed it, then retrieved it after it was shot.

THE NEW WORLD

On the other side of the ocean, the indigenous people of the Americas also shared their lives with several varieties of native dogs. In South America, the Toltecs as early as the ninth century A.D. and later the Aztecs bred dogs for both companionship and for food.

The Indians of North America kept dingo/coyotelike dogs as workers and companions. As many as ten dogs per family served variously as babysitters, guards, fishing assistants, hunters, and bed-warmers; dogs even wore backpacks and dragged goods-filled travois. The Salish people of the Pacific Northwest also kept luxuriantly furred "wool dogs," whose white coats were shorn and used to weave blankets and robes. Historians estimate the native dog population of North America was in the hundreds of thousands—until the Europeans arrived.

The Spanish conquistadores brought along Mastiffs and Greyhounds, referred to as "devouring dogs" by the natives because they were used primarily to hunt, attack, and subjugate the inhabitants. Columbus' second voyage included twenty European dogs that were used as food tasters and hunters of game and were themselves eaten when food was scarce.

The familiar dog breeds of Europe accompanied early settlers to America. Herding dogs helped manage the sheep and cattle, and hounds were highly prized. In 1650, Englishman Robert Brooke sailed for the Crown Colony in America with his pack of hounds, which are thought to have founded several strains of American hunters such as the American Foxhound. However, the local canine population's resemblance to wild coyotes made early European settlers uncomfortable, so they systematically killed native American dogs to near extinction by 1900.

As early settlers pioneered the new country, they needed versatile dogs that could hunt varmints, track game, herd livestock, and protect the homestead. New breeds evolved, some by accident and others by design. For instance, the Black Mouth Cur (Old Yeller is an example) was a result of breeding European dogs, native American dogs, and Spanish Mastiffs. The Catahoula Leopard Dog (official state dog of Louisiana) is thought to have been developed by the Catahoula Indians by breeding Spanish war dogs with red wolves.

The cat's fortunes had also changed by the sixteenth century, and cats were widespread in Europe where enlightened individuals began to take an interest in them. While dog fanciers prized canine function, cat fanciers cherished feline beauty; unique cat varieties were bred and pampered, and travelers brought back odd examples from around the world. The first recorded cat show to display the cat varieties of the day took place in Winchester, England, in 1598. But America's love affair with purebred cats came much later.

It's not clear when domestic cats arrived in the New World. The early Toltec and Aztec societies of South America revered the jaguar, which figured in their religious beliefs, but domestic cats were introduced much later by Europeans. As the companions of sailors, it's likely that cats accompanied the earliest travelers—perhaps the Skogkatt (Norwegian Forest Cat) with the Vikings, or even a European Shorthair or two with the Pilgrims on the Mayflower—to North America. But cats remained precious commodities for some time, prized for their vermin-catching ability and jealously guarded by seafaring travelers. Those cats that jumped ship to make their homes with early settlers were the domestic cats of Europe, similar to the modern British Shorthair or France's blue cat, the Chartreux. It was likely these or similar cats that were imported in 1749 to attack a plague of black rats in Pennsylvania. From these early cat pioneers sprang the American Shorthair, which served as farm cat, city cat, and pet.

America's semi-cobby shorthair cat remained the same for some time. But ships from around the world carried exotic longhaired cats like the Persian and Ankora (Turkish Angora), whose influence—along with perhaps the local Lynx or Bobcat—introduced new genes into the mix. The origination of America's own cat breed, the Maine Coon, is steeped in myth, but likely resulted from this genetic hash. More variety was introduced when the Oriental-type Siamese and Abyssinian arrived first in Great Britain, and then America, in the 1800s. But however beautiful, cats (like dogs) continued to work for a living, until their owners' own lifestyle changed.

PETS ARRIVE

By the mid-1800s, more than half of England's population lived in cities for the first time, and American society also began to shift from a primarily agricultural to an industrial basis. Consequently, people began to keep dogs of all sizes and varieties strictly as pets. Entertainment of the eighteenth century, which had included bear-baiting, hunting, and dogfights, began to be replaced by more civilized pursuits. The first anticruelty societies were formed to protect dogs, cats, horses, and other domestic animals from the insults of man.

The domestication of cats also took a step forward in the nineteenth century as people began breeding cats to specified standards. In 1871 London's Crystal Palace was the site of a formal exhibition of various cat breeds, particularly British Shorthair and Persian cats. And in 1895 the first American cat show was held at Madison Square Garden in New York City. Two hundred cats were entered and competed during the four-day show, won by a brown tabby Maine Coon.

But it wasn't until the 1960s that cats truly secured their role as pets in both America and Europe. Until then cats were typically the lesser-loved stepchildren, welcomed indoors for brief periods, but then put out at night because even cat lovers had trouble dealing with the cat's bathroom habits. The indoor cat's toilet facilities typically consisted of a box filled with ashes, sand, or sawdust—a smelly and messy affair. The innovation of cat litter, first marketed in the early 1960s in America, literally brought the cat from the farmyard into the parlor, and Kitty hasn't left since.

The 1970s witnessed a surge in feline popularity. Until then veterinarians had treated cats just like dogs, which they understood much better. But as cats became better known and more closely studied, great strides were made in their medical care and treatment.

Cats and dogs are now nearly equal in their popularity among Americans. More households keep dogs, but because many people own several felines, there are more pet cats than dogs.

As long as nature experiments and people find the changes enriching, the domestication process will continue. But just as the human hand has changed the way dogs and cats behave, live, and look, the association with these creatures has changed people in profound ways as well.

REDEFINING SERVICE

Cats and dogs have historically been put to wide use in the service of man, and they have faithfully fulfilled their roles as hunters and guardians. Dogs have also served as shepherds and draft animals and, more recently, have used their extraordinary scenting abilities to sniff out drugs, explosives, even termites.

But in the last quarter of the twentieth century, cats and dogs have broken the traditional boundaries of domestication to achieve unprecedented status among humans in the Western world. Cats and dogs are more than just companions; in some cases, they are literally extensions of their human partner, becoming surrogate hands, eyes, and ears. This evolution of pet purpose has redefined the human-pet relationship and our expectations of our cats' and dogs' potentials. When pets happily meet such challenges as service animals, building a peaceable kingdom with both seems a reasonable, more attainable goal.

The concept of service animals was born shortly after World War I in Germany, when soldiers blinded during the conflict were partnered with dogs trained to be their eyes. The idea quickly spread to other countries. German Shepherd breeder Bonnie Eustace trained the first American guide dog in 1928.

Much more recently, signal animals have entered the arena and pricked up their ears in service to the deaf. Because they typically alert through touch by jumping upon or against their masters, smaller dogs are usually used as signal animals. They alert their partners to such sounds as fire alarms, a doorbell, a crying baby, and an alarm clock. Although cats are not routinely trained, many felines also learn to serve as ears for their human partners.

Dogs have been asked to lend their paws in other service areas, too. These dogs pull wheelchairs, provide a sturdy support, and serve those who have limited or no use of their hands by retrieving and delivering objects, picking up the phone, turning lights on and off, and even helping people get dressed.

THE NEXT GENERATION

Although their smaller size precludes cats from serving in certain capacities, the animal service field of recent years has recognized endless possibilities for cats as well as other species. Pets closely attuned to their partners have learned to warn of impending seizures, debilitating headaches, and even heart attacks in time for their companion to take lifesaving medication or to seek help.

Animal-assisted therapy was the next logical step in pet service. This concept took off in the 1980s and opened the doors of hospitals and nursing homes to cats and dogs. There, animals serve as furry complements to regular therapy, helping patients deal with physical, emotional, and psychological difficulties.

The use of animals for therapeutic purposes is actually ancient, however. One of the earliest recorded programs began in the ninth century in Geel, Belgium, where caring for farm animals was prescribed to help "reestablish the harmony of soul and body" as a treatment for people with disabilities.

Today cats and dogs of all shapes and sizes, chosen for their calm, even temperaments, are used in every therapeutic setting imaginable. Their presence and nonjudgmental affection help countless people suffering from a wide range of difficulties, from clinical depression and schizophrenia to traumatic injury, AIDS, and age-related infirmities. Children and adults who are reluctant to endure uncomfortable rehabilitation go the extra mile willingly when the treatment includes interaction with a pet.

Somehow that cold nose or purring presence makes the ordeal easier to bear. Cats and dogs prompt smiles, first words, and a return of hope to emotionally damaged people who cannot be reached in any other way.

Why should petting a cat or throwing Poochie a ball inspire such miracles in these people? People have become isolated, deprived of human contact, in the last few decades. In the past, psychologists claimed that people responded strongly to the affection of cats and dogs because they were replacement objects that fulfilled our frustrated need to nurture. But more recent medical opinion acknowledges that, for most of us, cats and dogs do not replace human relationships; they *promote* them. Pets serve as an emotional and social bridge among people. Therapy animals are successful because they prompt interaction, emotion, and dialogue, which can then be guided and interpreted by the human therapist.

This recognition of the importance of pets in human interaction has led to a new type of service animal called the social animal. These cats and dogs—or ferrets, lizards, or other pets—serve as a social lubricant between the human partner and other people.

Social animals are particularly helpful for children who are perceived by their peers to be "different" in some way and who therefore have difficulty interacting. The dog or cat that accompanies the child supplants the child's special needs as the focus of attention during encounters with others. The animal is the bridge that links these children to their peers, helping to normalize social interaction.

PETS ARE GOOD FOR US

People have always known, consciously or otherwise, that keeping cats and dogs makes us feel good. Why else would more than 66.2 million cats and 58 million dogs be kept by Americans? But scientists wanted measurable evidence before they would agree to the obvious.

In fact, a number of very specific health benefits have been identified and validated by recent scientific studies. For example, people suffering from heart disease survive longer if they have a pet; the nearness of a cat or dog reduces stress by measurably lowering blood pressure. Elderly people who have pets are emotionally and physically healthier because pets keep them connected to life. Such people don't need to see the doctor as often, and they require less medication. When treatment is required, people with pets recover more quickly. Dogs and cats are not only fun to have around, they help keep us healthy.

CHAPTER THREE

Pet Considerations

By domesticating cats and dogs, we have changed them irrevocably. They are dependent upon us for food, shelter, companionship, and, yes, even a reason to live. Pets have given us so much, always with a happy wag or a satisfied purr, that providing for their proper care is only just.

Individual pet situations vary depending on the kind of household in which a pet lives and the amount of space that's available. Is your home a high-rise apartment? A house in the suburbs? A farmhouse in the country? Are all of your pets under one roof, or do they share a fenced yard or have acres to romp?

Even the other people who share your house, and the time that they can spend with the dog or cat, will affect interspecies relationships. Are you a single person, a retired couple, or a member of a young family with many children?

Living with cats and dogs together can, without the proper preparations, result in bedlam. Cats don't act like dogs, nor do they react to the same things or in the same way. Dogs and cats require very different grooming and health care. And both species have distinctive ideas about what they want out of life.

Most problems develop when people try to care for cats and dogs together in the same home without fully understanding both and appreciating the differences between them. Applying the principles of canine care to cats, or of feline care to dogs, could at a minimum result in catastrophic behavior problems or, at worst, the death of your pet.

With the proper preparations, all dogs and cats have the potential to live together peaceably. However, certain animals seem to be more agreeable to interspecies relationships than others, and choosing pets with these tendencies goes a long way toward promoting harmony in the home.

Obviously, cats and dogs can vary greatly in size. Even the friendliest, gentlest of big bruiser pets may accidentally injure one that's much smaller. Although Mutt and Jeff friendships may blossom, great care must be taken, at least initially, when there is a large size difference between pets.

Feline breeds vary in size from about 3 pounds in the Singapura to more than 20 pounds in the Ragdoll and some Maine Coon cats. Non-pedigreed felines run the gamut from tiny to big. A confident cat that has the muscle to back up his threats can make life miserable for—or even threaten the life of—a tiny puppy or a diminutive adult dog.

Canine breeds offer an even wider range in dimensions, from the teacup-size Japanese Chin and Chihuahua, which weigh only a few pounds each, to the giant breeds. The Irish Wolfhound, Great Dane, and Mastiff are among the largest; some dogs have been known to weigh well over 200 pounds and may be taller than a person when standing on their hind legs.

A small cat may look like a midnight snack to these big dogs. Other dogs, though often gentle, may become unintentionally rough in play and injure the much smaller kitten or cat simply by swatting it, stepping on it, or sitting on it.

PET PERSONALITY

Even more important than size is the specific pet's personality. Individual cat and dog personalities can be as varied as the patterns of a kaleidoscope. Generally, three measures of personality will have the greatest impact on pet compatibility. They are dominance; fear or anxiety; and predatory behavior.

Dominance refers to a "me first" attitude that is sometimes characterized by belligerence and a tendency to do whatever's necessary to get one's own way. It is measured in relationship to a pet's rank within the social group, which, for purposes of this book, includes the whole family of cats, dogs, and people living under the same roof.

Cats and dogs have very different ideas about rank (more

about this in Chapter 12). Problems arise when the dog and the cat struggle to assert dominance and neither will offer to submit. Both insist on being the leader, and neither will agree to be the follower. When the desire for dominance is thwarted, the pets' frustration and constant struggle to establish their place within the family group may escalate to aggression.

A cat or dog will experience fear or anxiety in response to perceived danger. This can occur when what the pet expects to experience is very different from what actually takes place or when the pet feels threatened by the presence or interference of another animal. A fearful pet that faces an extremely dominant pet will typically react in one of two ways: either it will withdraw and attempt to hide or it will defend itself and try to take back control of its destiny by becoming hostile.

The pet that experiences fear or anxiety is not necessarily the smallest or youngest. In fact, it's often the older pet stressed by the infirmities of age that is fearful or anxious when confronted by a belligerent or pushy youngster. It's not unusual for a big but frail old dog to be intimidated by a robust, in-your-face kitten. Although it may look comical to us when Junior Cat chases King Dog around the house, to the dog this is no laughing matter.

The third measure of personality—predatory behavior—is particularly important as it relates to dominance. The urge to hunt, capture, and kill prey is innate in most predators, even those that have been domesticated for many thousands of years. All cats and dogs, to one degree or another, exhibit certain types of predatory behavior.

Every cat is inherently a predatory creature, whether it hunts mice, moths, or string. The urge to strike out with claws and capture and bite the moving object is hot-wired into the feline brain. It's not hunger so much as motion or sound that stimulates this behavior. The cry or the scampering movement of a tiny puppy may trigger predatory action in a dominant cat if the cat isn't taught to temper this instinctive response.

In some dogs, predatory behavior has been modified and redirected. Herding breeds, for example, dominate sheep or cows by driving or chasing them, perhaps nipping at their heels to keep them moving. They show the normal predatory behavior patterns of stalking, staring, and chasing, but they stop short of attacking and killing. Dogs bred for protection, on the other hand, may identify so closely with their owners that they may perceive any interloper as a threat and launch an attack.

Hunting dogs have refined predatory behavior to an art. Pointers and setters have been developed to locate prey, and that's all; they stalk, but they don't chase or attack. Retrievers bring back the prey killed by the human hunter, while spaniels chase or flush prey from hiding places into the open for the hunter to kill, and then retrieve it. And hounds are trackers that stalk their prey by scent or sight.

Terriers were developed to catch and kill vermin, including rats or mice, or larger varmints like foxes, badgers, and weasels. These breeds, from large to small, react to moving objects much as cats do.

Whatever the breed, canine predatory behavior is apparent in the actions of chasing a ball, retrieving a stick, playing tug-of-war, or shaking a towel to death. When this behavior is strong in a dominant dog, the risk to the cat increases, unless the dog can be made to understand that Kitty is neither for play nor for prey.

KEEPING THE PEACE

Socializing your pet—helping the animal learn appropriate behavior—is the single most important step toward ensuring a peaceable kingdom. Proper socialization prepares cats and dogs not only to accept but to get along well with other members of their own species.

Proper socialization teaches a cat how to be a cat, what is proper feline etiquette, how to communicate with other felines, and who the cat's friends and enemies are. In the same way, dogs develop canine social and communication skills and learn to identify acceptable and unacceptable members of the canine clan.

Domestication has changed cats and dogs in many ways, but perhaps the most important has to do with socialization. Unlike most other mammals, dogs and cats can be socialized to their own species and to other species at the same time. This means they can be taught to recognize people as well as other pets as acceptable members of their family.

The greatest problems occur when cats and dogs are forced to live together without having been properly socialized to each other. Poorly socialized cats and dogs aren't able to relax and enjoy themselves; they are constantly under stress. They may perceive unfamiliar animals or people as a threat, and this could result in a fear reaction or predatory behavior or a combination of the two.

If such dogs and cats are unable to bond closely with their owner or their extended family, they may make life miserable for everyone. Sadly, the poorly socialized cat's or dog's behavior is often so disruptive that he loses his home and any chance of happiness. In fact, cats and dogs that have no contact with people during the critical socialization period will not experience normal interactions with people; instead they will react like wild creatures.

PROMOTING THE PEOPLE-PET CONNECTION

Well-adjusted pets enjoy interacting with their human family as well as with the other furry members of the group. Proper socialization fosters a high degree of trust between the pet and the owner. This willingness to trust and submit to people is necessary if the cat or dog is to receive proper care.

Socialization not only improves trainability but also stimulates problem-solving abilities in cats and dogs. Well-socialized pets are more confident and don't need to be dominant in order to feel secure. They are less fearful, and they adjust more quickly when faced with novel situations.

Although cats and dogs can be "reprogrammed" to a certain extent at any age, they are most amenable to socialization during kitten- or puppyhood. It is during this time that the most effective bonding with people and other animals takes place and they are prepared to accept new and unexpected situations.

Events that furry babies experience are most likely to have a long-term effect on their development if they occur at a young age. For dogs, the most sensitive period begins in the fourth week of life and lasts to about ten weeks of age. The comparable period for kittens begins and ends earlier than in dogs, from the end of the second week of life through about seven weeks of age.

Kittens and puppies play-fight at the beginning of this socialization period. This activity teaches them to inhibit their use of tooth and claw. It also helps them develop coordination, and it allows them to explore and learn about their world. The first dominance hierarchies are established among puppies from eight to nine weeks old, but these can change as a dog matures.

Puppies and kittens are best socialized to live with others of their own species if they stay with their mother and siblings throughout the socialization period—until ten to twelve weeks of age is a good rule of thumb. In puppies, the most sensitive period in establishing relationships with people is between six and eight weeks of age, while in kittens it is two to seven weeks of age.

People who raise puppies or kittens must take a hand in properly socializing the youngsters in order to ensure happy pets. Regular handling of the babies—picking them up, holding them, playing with them, grooming them, and physically interacting with them in other ways—is imperative for healthy socialization. Twenty to sixty minutes daily seems to produce the best results, particularly if interaction takes place in the presence of the littermates and the mother. This makes a strange situation more familiar and less threatening. Talking while handling the puppies or kittens makes a strong impression and creates a strong bond, perhaps because it prepares the babies to respond to human communication.

Because young pets often go to their new homes in the middle of this highly impressionable period, owners must ensure that proper socialization continues. The new owner should expose the puppy or kitten to a wide range of experiences during this period. You can introduce the youngster to a variety of social situations, such as groups of people, noisy children, or traveling in a car. Young pets should become familiar with grooming and bathing equipment, training tools like collars and leashes, and routine care. Each new situation they face and overcome will build their confidence so that they can better handle unique, unexpected, or stressful situations in the future.

Young puppies and kittens that experience a wide range of people and other pets are more likely to live peaceably together as adults. They are usually less frightened or stressed by a stranger later in life. This is particularly important when a single person adopts a puppy or kitten and plans to marry and have children at some point during the pet's future.

It is also during the socialization period that puppies and kittens learn to identify dangerous people, animals, and objects. Basically they "imprint" a traumatic incident, and use it as a template to process future experiences. A kitten that is chased by a noisy canine may never accept dogs, even friendly ones, just as a child who is frightened by one dog may thereafter fear all dogs.

Try to create fond memories and pave the way to future tranquillity by ensuring that the puppy's early encounters with cats, and the kitten's first experiences with dogs, are pleasant ones. Expose your impressionable youngster to gentle cats and dogs that already accept each other. That way, the young kitten that is introduced to a gentle dog will perceive canines as a normal part of life and will be more likely to accept dogs in the future. And puppies introduced to accommodating adult cats will learn to respect and accept felines as a part of their social group.

But as in any relationship, there can be trouble in paradise. By understanding the basic differences between dogs and cats and applying that knowledge to your own circumstances, you can avoid problems and smooth out the bumps that may appear along the way.

PART TWO

Cats Are from Venus, Dogs Are from Mars

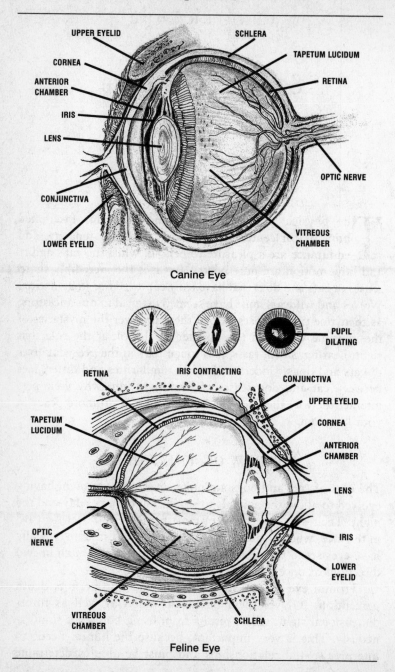

UPPER EYELID
SCHLERA
CORNEA
TAPETUM LUCIDUM
ANTERIOR CHAMBER
RETINA
IRIS
LENS
OPTIC NERVE
CONJUNCTIVA
LOWER EYELID
VITREOUS CHAMBER

Canine Eye

PUPIL DILATING
IRIS CONTRACTING

RETINA
CONJUNCTIVA
UPPER EYELID
CORNEA
TAPETUM LUCIDUM
ANTERIOR CHAMBER
LENS
IRIS
OPTIC NERVE
LOWER EYELID
VITREOUS CHAMBER
SCHLERA

Feline Eye

CHAPTER FOUR

Seeing Eye to Eye

The physical prowess of cats and dogs has fascinated humans for centuries. The dog's strength, tenacity, and endurance are a pleasure to behold, while the cat's agility and lithe motion are pure poetry. But it is the incredibly sharp senses of cats and dogs that have truly captured our imagination. Wolves and wildcats must have seemed magical to our ancestors, as their fine-tuned senses helped them uncover the mysteries of the invisible world. In this chapter we'll look at the role that sight, hearing, smell, taste, and touch play in the everyday lives of cats and dogs. Understanding the similarities and differences between cat and dog senses offers insight into why your pets interact the way they do, which can help you promote peace in your kingdom.

WINDOW ON THE WORLD

The eyes of cats and dogs are quite similar to our own, having evolved to allow the animals to see during both the day and the night. Their eyes, like those of most predators, are set forward in the face, whereas prey animals like deer and rabbits typically have eyes set in the sides of the head so they can watch in two directions at once.

Frontal eye placement in the cat and dog permits depth perception. It gives them binocular vision as well as three-dimensional sight, which results from using both eyes simultaneously. This is very important, because the hunter needs to interpret spatial relationships and must be able to determine how far away he is from his quarry in order to correctly time his pursuit or pounce.

Eye placement varies quite a bit between flat-faced and narrow-headed dog breeds. For instance, the Afghan Hound's eyes tend to be closer to the sides of the face than those of the Boston Terrier. In general, dogs have a greater field of vision than do cats, but cats have a wider range of binocular vision. The dog's binocular vision is less than half that of people.

Cats are experts at seeing motion from the corners of their eyes—your dog will notice it's quite difficult to sneak up on a cat—and this peripheral vision comes in handy when they are hunting. The cat has the largest eyes of any meat eater; if our own eyes were proportionally the same as the cat's, human eyes would be 8 inches across. Compared with humans, cats and dogs see the world in a blur.

The eyes of cats and dogs work essentially the same way as ours do. Light passes through the clear windowlike cornea on the front surface of the eye, moves on through the dark opening called the pupil, and enters the lens, which focuses the light images onto the retina at the back of the eye. Unlike humans, all dogs and cats have a third eyelid called the haw, or nictitating membrane, located in the inner corner of the eye. More prominent in some breeds than in others, it acts as a windshield wiper that sweeps horizontally across the eye.

The iris mechanism, the colored portion of the eye, is a muscle that opens the pupil into a wide circle to allow in maximum illumination during low light conditions. In bright light, the dog's iris contracts the pupil to a pinpoint that limits the amount allowed inside. The iris in the feline eye, on the other hand, is a more complex figure-eight muscle; it can close much farther than that of the canine eye, giving the cat's eye added protection. In bright light, the cat's iris closes the pupil to a vertical slit. The cat can use its eyelids to reduce the amount of light even further by squinting; this also helps the cat to focus on images.

The retina, which acts like a movie screen, is covered with highly specialized light-receptor cells. Cones recognize color, and rods respond to shades of black and white. Dogs and cats have many more rods than people do and so have much better vision in lower light. Cats require only one-sixth as much illumination as we do and use twice as much available light. Dogs' eyes are about half as efficient as cats', but they are still better at using light than humans.

Both cats and dogs also have a tapetum lucidum, a layer of highly reflective cells behind the retina, which enhances the light-gathering efficiency of their eyes by about 40 percent. When the reflection escapes through the pupil at night, you can see an eerie night-shine from your pet's eyes.

For years experts have debated whether or not cats and dogs can see color, and many books will state that animals are color-blind and can only detect shades of gray. However, both animals do have the equipment—cones—to distinguish between certain colors, and recent studies confirm that dogs and cats do indeed see color. It has been determined, however, that our pets' color sense is based on a dichromatic, or two-color, system (blue and green) rather than the three-color system (red, yellow, and blue) of primates and humans. In very bright light, green and blue seem much brighter than red to cats and dogs, because they have very few red-sensitive cones or none at all. Feline daytime vision is dominated by shades of blue.

SOUND SENSE

Dogs and cats both have extraordinary hearing ability. They can hear sounds that humans cannot detect, and both use their auditory sense to stay in touch with their environment. The ear structure of cats and dogs is remarkably similar; both have an outer ear, a middle ear, and an inner ear where hearing actually takes place.

The outside ear, which you can see, is referred to as the pinna. It's made of cartilage and covered with skin and fur. This outer ear is extremely mobile, with a multitude of muscles that allow it to be swiveled as much as 180 degrees. The pinna is a kind of funnel that collects and amplifies sound waves and directs them down the auditory canal into the middle ear. In people, this canal is straight, but in dogs and cats it's shaped more like an L running straight down from the pinna, with the foot of the L angling inward. This two-directional canal helps protect the inner structures of the ear from injury.

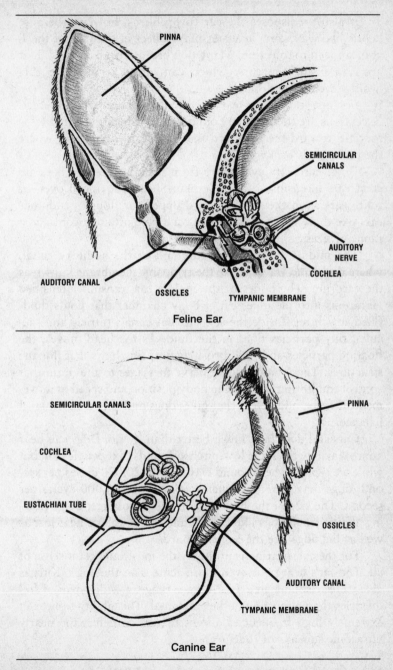

PINNA

SEMICIRCULAR
CANALS

AUDITORY
NERVE

COCHLEA

AUDITORY CANAL   OSSICLES   TYMPANIC MEMBRANE

Feline Ear

SEMICIRCULAR CANALS

COCHLEA

EUSTACHIAN TUBE

PINNA

OSSICLES

AUDITORY CANAL

TYMPANIC MEMBRANE

Canine Ear

It also predisposes the ear to problems, however, because debris like wax, dirt, or water may collect in the foot of the *L* and can lead to infection. Many dog breeds also have thick hair growing inside the ears, which can make keeping the ears healthy even more difficult.

In cats, the outer ear is usually triangular and erect. Exceptions are the Scottish Fold breed, in which the pinna folds forward toward the face, and the American Curl breed, where the pinna curls backward.

Dogs' ears vary even more from breed to breed. There are erect ears like those of the German Shepherd, tipped over, or tulip, ears as in the Collie, and dropped, or floppy pendulous ears like those of the Beagle, and each type of pinna comes in a range of sizes.

The middle ear begins at the end of the auditory canal, where the sound waves strike the tympanic membrane known as the eardrum. The bones of the middle ear transmit intensified vibrations into the inner ear, a bony chamber that holds fluid-filled structures. Inside the semicircular canals (utricle and saccule), tiny particles float in the fluid. As the head moves, the floating particles and fluid brush against tiny hairs that line the structures. These hairs trigger nerve messages to the brain that control equilibrium and define body position and speed of movement. It is the middle ear that gives dogs and cats their sense of balance.

Cats and dogs hear much better than we do. Dogs can hear approximately the same low-pitched sounds that people can, but while we typically hear sound waves up to 20,000 cycles per second, dogs may hear frequencies as high as 100,000 cycles per second. The size of the breed doesn't seem to affect dogs' hearing ability; small dogs like Dachshunds seem able to hear just as well as big dogs like the Saint Bernard.

For the cat, hearing is probably the most important sense of all. The cat's hearing is even more acute than the dog's. Kitty is able to hear sounds in a 10.5-octave range, a wider span of frequencies than almost any other mammal. This ability to hear in extremely high frequencies allows the cat to detect the nearly ultrasonic squeaks of rodent prey.

SCENT CONNOISSEURS

The sense of smell is a defining factor in the lives of cats and, especially, of dogs, who rely most heavily on their scenting ability. The canine sense of smell is far more acute than that of humans.

For cats and dogs, a scent is like a name tag that allows them to distinguish friend from foe, to gather sexual information, to communicate, and to interact socially.

Humans have between 5 and 20 million scent-analyzing cells, compared to the cat's typical 67 million. Canine scent sense varies from one breed to another. The Dachshund, for instance, has about 125 million such cells, compared to the German Shepherd's 200 million. The best canine sniffer of them all—the Bloodhound—is believed to have 300 million olfactory cells.

The shape and size of the external nose varies greatly between breeds of cats and dogs. Overall, the cat has a much shorter muzzle than the dog, although breeds like the Siamese have muzzles as much as two inches longer than the flatter-faced Persian-type breeds. Similarly, the long, pointed muzzle of a dog breed like the Poodle contrasts with the flat-faced profile of the Pug.

In general, a long muzzle accommodates more scent-detecting equipment, which is why dogs have a much more highly developed sense of smell than cats. That's also why longer-nosed dog breeds tend to be better sniffers than the flat-faced varieties; nonetheless, all dogs and cats are quite adept at smell detection.

The hairless end of the nose, referred to as the leather, contains the nostrils, through which airborne scent enters the nose. The nostrils open into the nasal cavity, which is enclosed in bone and cartilage and runs the length of the muzzle. The nasal cavity empties into the throat behind the soft palate. Sinuses, which are open spaces in the bone, are connected to the nasal cavity and help shape the barks and whines, meows and purrs, of dogs and cats.

The nasal cavity is divided by a midline partition into two halves, one for each nostril. Called the nasal septum, this divider is made of bone and cartilage and lined by a mucous membrane. A series of scrolled bony plates, called turbinates, are located

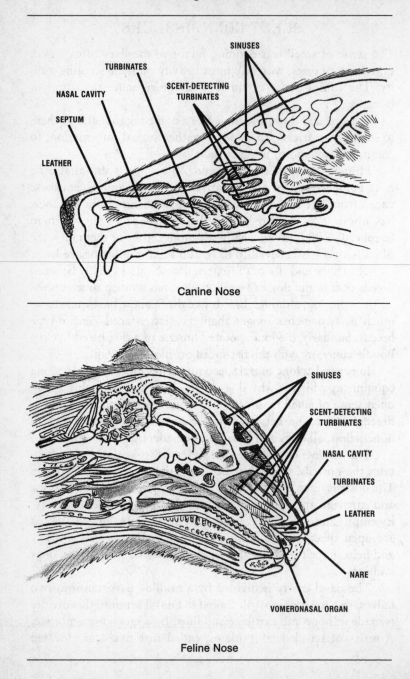

Canine Nose

Feline Nose

inside the nasal cavity. Useful for smelling the world, they also protect the dog and cat by cleaning, warming, and humidifying air as the pet inhales.

These protective structures are situated in the front portion of the nasal cavity and are more highly developed in the dog than in the cat. That's probably because cats exert themselves and breathe heavily only for brief spans of time, while dogs are much more active over longer periods during which they must breathe more rapidly. The highly developed warming areas in the dog's nose give the air more time to be screened before passing on to the sensitive scent-detecting portions.

The turbinates are covered by a thick, spongy membrane called the olfactory mucosa, which contains the scent-detecting nerves and cells. Depending on the breed, dogs have from 7 to 60 square inches of olfactory mucosa, compared to the cat's 8 square inches and the human's 1 square inch.

Odor particles inhaled by the dog or cat are first dissolved in the moist layer of mucus that coats the inside of the nose. Millions of microscopic hairlike receptors sprout from the olfactory cells up into this thin layer of mucus. When an odor particle comes in contact with the receptor, it is fed down to the olfactory cell, which in turn is somehow excited by the odor.

Cats and dogs have another pair of scent-detecting organs that people do not have. Called the Jacobson's organs, or vomeronasal organs, they are thought to detect sex-linked scents. These organs are fluid-filled sacs located between the hard palate in the roof of the mouth and the nasal septum. Tiny ducts connect the sacs to the inside of the mouth directly behind the front teeth, then continue up into the nasal cavity.

It is their preoccupation with scent that prompts dogs to roll in malodorous stuff, the smellier the better. (Our family's Shetland Sheepdog, Lady, was anything *but* a lady when she rolled in ripe carp that floated onto the riverbank.) Dogs delight in rolling in anything from garbage to fresh cow droppings. When they find a noxious aroma, dogs dab it on like a woman splashing herself with perfume. It's theorized that taking on a gamy odor allows the dog to carry home scent messages to pack members about his travels.

Cats also roll in fragrant stuff, but their scent fascination is with catnip, a member of the mint family that is a kind of feline hallucinogen. When catnip is rolled on and bitten, it releases a volatile oil that gives some cats an instant high. Affected cats act like furry fools as they drool and flop about. Catnip is a harmless indulgence that affects only two out of three cats, and overuse can dull the effect. Catnip can also serve as an effective training tool for cats.

A TOUCHING RELATIONSHIP

Dogs and cats relish the sensation of a stroking hand. Touch is one of the first sensations newborn puppies and kittens experience as their mothers wash them. Contact with other creatures provides an emotional link between them and may also be a component of communication.

Both cats and dogs have distinct types of nerve sensors located in the skin and scattered over much of the body. Nerves called mechanoreceptors are found near the base of each hair, especially the whiskers, and respond to skin movement. Direct contact or even something touching the hair can cause a response; sensors in the footpads detect vibration from the ground.

Temperature is detected by specialized thermoreceptors; some react to cold while others respond to heat. Cats in particular love the sensation of warmth and tend to seek out sunny perches. Dogs have an unusual cold receptor on their lips, which cats do not have. Perhaps this tells dogs whether or not food is the proper temperature to eat.

Another kind of nerve, the nociceptor, is sensitive to pain. Certain nociceptors respond to mechanical stimulation like crushing or squeezing of the skin, while others are sensitive to extremes of temperature. Dogs and cats experience pain in the same way that we do. However, their nerves reach a maximum response level before true pain is reached, which means it's hard for the cat and dog to tell the difference between a strong, uncomfortable sensation and one that is dangerous. Cats, for instance, can tolerate temperatures up to 126°F. before registering pain. A love of warmth may prompt them to sleep too near

the fireplace and risk singeing their fur or even being burned
before they realize they've been hurt.

In both dogs and cats, the sense of touch is most sensitive in
the area surrounding the muzzle. Cats also have particularly sensitive footpads, which can detect differences in temperature of
only a degree or two. This heat sense helps newborn animals find
their mother.

A MATTER OF TASTE

The sense of taste for dogs and cats is thought to be similar to
our own, in which the sensation of flavor is produced by a combination of the taste and the smell of food. Taste buds in both
dogs and cats are on the upper surface of the tongue, the roof of
the mouth, and the inside of the lips, and are designed to predispose them to foods that are essential for their health.

Both cats and dogs can detect bitter, acidic, sweet, and sour
tastes. The cat tends to reject those flavors that accumulate in
the tissues of animals after they have died, and experts believe
this may account for the cat's rejection of carrion as food. Yet
for cats, certain amino acids in meat trigger a sweet flavor that
they love. But Kitty has no taste for sugar at all.

Dogs, however, have a well-known sweet tooth triggered by
many of the same sugary substances that people like. Able to
subsist on fruits and vegetables, the dog has retained an ability
to detect sweet-tasting compounds including sugar. The sweet-
ness of foods indicates the presence of highly digestible energy,
so the ability to respond to sweet flavors encourages dogs to eat
these foods.

Salt can enhance other flavors in foods, but neither cats nor
dogs appear to have a *specific* response to salt. This may be
because wild carnivores obtain salt naturally by eating other animals; they don't need to find a salt lick, as herbivores like cows
and horses do.

The gustatory sense can, however, get our dogs and cats in
trouble. Cats have a reputation as finicky eaters, probably due
to their preference for strong flavors, particularly fish. They can
develop an addiction to certain foods, which can jeopardize their

health if the preferred food isn't complete and balanced and the cat refuses to eat anything else.

Dogs tend to have the opposite problem. Some dogs will eat anything, anywhere, whether it's moving or not. This less than discriminatory eating behavior leads Poochie to eat from the garbage can and the candy dish, and even to gobble down inedible items. My grandmother used to scrape the dinner plates with a paper napkin before washing the dishes, and her dog would rescue the gravy-soaked paper from the trash and eat it with relish.

The similarities and differences between cat and dog senses influence their behavior. These senses determine the way they react to their world, including their interaction with people and with each other.

CHAPTER FIVE

To Chase or to Ambush

The way cats and dogs react to each other and to the world around them depends on how their bodies function. This chapter compares feline and canine structure, describes how each species uses claws and teeth, muscles and senses, and explains why an animal's physique and behavior are interrelated.

SNIFFING MACHINES

Winston, a black-and-tan Basset Hound, lives through his nose. He spends all his outdoor time sniffing and snorting every square inch of ground. Ever since his owners brought Bickers the cat home to keep him company, Winston has enjoyed his time indoors even more. Bickers is constantly on the move, from one hiding place to another, while Winston delightedly sniffs him out. The dog's short legs allow him to scramble into tight spots, and only Bickers's great climbing ability keeps him beyond Winston's rude nose. For dogs like Winston, scent is a narcotic that drives them to distraction; they let nothing stand in the way of a really good sniff.

Like their wolf forebears, dogs depend on sensory information when hunting; they use scent to identify and to locate prey. Many hunting breeds use their exquisite sense of smell to track game over long distances. Some dogs track using a nose-to-the-ground approach. The long muzzle of these breeds equips them with more scent-detecting equipment and makes it easier for them to sniff the ground. When they put their noses to the ground, their pendulous ears and the loose skin of their jowls fall forward and actually direct the scent-saturated air to their nose. Some hunting dogs like the Black and Tan Coonhound also "give voice," loudly announcing the location of the animal with woofs, barks, and bays, keeping the human partner apprised of their progress.

When cats and dogs live together in the same house, it's nearly impossible for Kitty to have any privacy because scent sense keeps Poochie informed of the cat's whereabouts, even if Kitty tries to hide. If your dog is bothering Kitty in this way, offer Poochie an alternative. Scenting games are great fun for dogs; play hide-and-seek with his favorite toy or old sock after scenting it with a bit of his favorite treat. First let him see you hide it; then reward him when he digs it out from beneath the sofa. Use a command like "Find it" or "Where's your ball" every time.

THE EYES HAVE IT

Cats rely more on sight and hearing than on scent. In fact, it is not hunger but motion that triggers predatory behavior in cats. That's why cats may seem preoccupied with a dog's waving tail and may drive Poochie to distraction trying to capture it.

Sight-hunting dogs like the Afghan Hound, Saluki, and Greyhound resemble cats in that they also rely more on sight than scent to find their prey. These dogs use their incredible speed—a sustained 35 miles an hour in Greyhounds—and great stamina to chase and run down game.

FELINE STEALTH VERSUS DOGGED PURSUIT

The impulse to pursue is deeply ingrained in dogs. Just as the motion of a mouse triggers a cat's desire to pounce, the fleeing cat stimulates Poochie's chase reflex. Dogs also chase sticks and balls, and even yearn after birds they haven't a hope of catching. It's this same instinct that causes some dogs to chase cars, risking injury or death.

Cats have very little endurance compared to dogs. While dogs enjoy hour-long walks and romps, and the ill-mannered among them even pull and tug at the leash to continue on, cats become exhausted in less than twenty minutes even at a leisurely pace. On a straightaway, the diligent dog will catch the cat every time.

Cats rely on slow, patient stealth with carefully timed short bursts of speed. Although some cats can run up to 30 miles an hour, they can sustain such speeds for only a very short dash, and they usually save their energy for the last few moments of the hunt. Oftentimes Kitty will simply hide and wait for the prey to come to her. The cat remains motionless until the quarry ventures out, and then Kitty strikes with lightning speed. Other cats prefer to stalk their prey.

Some dogs have been bred and trained to have the patience of the cat once they have located their target. Border Collies use a distinctive stealthy stance, head lowered and eyes staring, to make their woolly charges do what they're told. When sheep aren't available to herd, the Border Collie will make do with what's at hand, nipping at the heels of children to round them up, or trying to herd the family cat.

Pointers and setters are trained to find game and then remain motionless once they've pointed it out to the hunter. But left to their own devices, many dogs will immediately flush the prey and begin a raucous pursuit. Cats and dogs living together may enjoy playing chasing games. Some cats actually invite the dog to race with outlandish teasing. But neither should be allowed to harass the other with unwanted chasing. Chapter 14 explains how to teach your pets the meaning of the word "no."

MOUTH AND PAW

Puppies put everything into their mouths, just as babies do, but dogs never outgrow the habit. Poochie doesn't have hands, so he uses his mouth to pick up and carry objects and explore his world. Dogs have great control over the strength of their bite and can be astoundingly gentle when they want to. Golden Retrievers can even be trained to carry a raw egg without breaking it.

This oral fixation may be frightening to a cat that doesn't expect it, but both creatures often adapt and take the situation in stride. I knew an Akita named Czar who liked to carry young kittens in his mouth. He never hurt them, and would spit them out wet and squirming whenever so commanded.

Cats are mouth-oriented in a different way. Although kittens mouth items as babies do, as they mature, their focus changes, and they use their mouths to keep themselves clean. Dogs may use their teeth to pull a stray burr out of their fur, but only the Basenji grooms itself with as much self-absorption as a cat.

The cat's grooming actually goes beyond cleanliness to serve a social function. Cats groom other cats, people, and even dogs that they consider a part of their family. This is a way of bonding, and a sharing of scent that makes everybody smell familiar and safe to the cat. It may be disconcerting to the uninitiated canine, but dogs ultimately love the attention and accept the feline massage.

Cats use their paws the way dogs use their mouths. Pats with an inquisitive paw educate the cat about that object. They also use their paws to educate others. Jake, a black Chow Chow, has learned to ignore his owner's cats. While still a puppy, Jake delighted in poking the big tabby, and Ginger put up with the rudeness as long as possible. After the first few pokes, Ginger gently patted the puppy's nose, but when that prompted Jake to poke even harder, the pats turned to sharp whacks. By the time Jake became a 65-pound adult, the 7-pound Ginger had him well trained not to stick his nose where it wasn't wanted.

The dog that inquisitively noses a cat should expect to feel a bop on the muzzle. When Kitty really means business, she'll use her claws.

TOOTH AND CLAW

Cats use their claws to scratch and groom themselves and as weapons for protection, defense, and attack. The cat can be a protective distance away and still reach out and touch—or slash—with dagger-sharp claws.

Backward-curving cat claws also serve as snares that catch and hold struggling prey. Cats are able to quickly scoop up small prey and flip them into the air, disorienting a mouse or a fish and thwarting its escape. House cats employ many of the same hunting techniques when playing with toys.

The cat who hunts will clutch her captured victim in both paws, hold it with her claws, and quickly dispatch it with a practiced bite. Cats use a killing bite to the back of the neck, just at the point where the head joins the backbone. Their specialized canine teeth—the long, pointed, dagger-shaped ones—are designed to separate a mouse's vertebrae and sever the spinal cord.

Most dogs are too large to be mistaken for feline prey, but they are often play targets for the cat. It's the canine toes, tail, and ears that most often attract Kitty's attention. Rough play may make the dog reluctant to interact further, or it may inspire canine aggression.

Dogs aren't able to use their paws with the same dexterity as cats. Instead, their mouths and teeth serve as their primary weapons. After locating prey and chasing it to exhaustion, the dog must draw near enough to grab it in his mouth. When the prey is smaller than the dog, he often seizes the victim's neck, like a cat. But instead of severing the spine, the dog uses his powerful jaws to hold the animal while he violently shakes his head to break its neck.

You'll often see dogs use this technique during play, fetching a Frisbee or ball until they drop from exhaustion, or savoring a game of tug-of-war with a towel. Once the dog wins the prize, he celebrates by vigorously shaking the towel as if trying to kill it.

Because of their size differences, dogs may easily switch into a predatory mode when faced with the movement of a cat. A dog's teeth can inflict great crushing and stabbing damage upon cats, but even worse is the bone-shattering action of being shaken.

Cats hunt alone out of necessity. Stealth requires solitude; the more individuals involved, the less likely it becomes that the hunter will remain invisible to the prey.

Dogs may hunt alone when the target is small game, but they often join forces when hunting larger prey such as deer or, sadly, sheep or calves. In these instances, they use the techniques of herding dogs to drive the prey into flight or to separate it from its herd. Sometimes a pair of dogs will chase the prey until they grow tired, and then another pair of dogs will join in, and the pack will chase in relays until the victim stops in exhaustion.

Because dogs must endanger themselves when they come within biting range, they have developed other defenses to help protect them from counterattack. Breeds like the Chinese Shar-Pei, for example, have developed a great deal of loose, elastic skin covered with bristly fur that's unpleasant to bite. Folds of extra flesh enable a Shar-Pei to literally move around inside his skin as if it were an organic bag. Even if an opponent latches on with his teeth, the Shar-Pei is able to turn around far enough to put his own fangs into play.

AFTER THE HUNT

Cats typically carry their prey to a hidden place where they feel safe before they settle down to eat the prize. This often means bringing fruits of the hunt into the house. Kitty may place her kill in a conspicuous place like the front step, your pillow, or at your feet, almost as if seeking praise. Some cats seem to look upon human owners as kittens that need to be fed.

Cats usually eat mice and other small animals whole. They may partially skin or pluck larger prey like blackbirds and bunnies and then consume the choice parts.

Dogs may carry small prey away, but they'll settle down and eat larger animals where they are killed. Their strong teeth and jaws allow them to crush and even consume some bones. While cats use their rough tongues to rasp tiny portions of flesh away from the bone, dogs use their teeth to gnaw it away.

When the urge to gnaw is thwarted, or when the dog is particularly bored, his chewing choices can drive owners to distraction. Clyde, a pound puppy with bird dog in his ancestry, took to chewing the baseboard in his owner's apartment, then moved on to the linoleum.

While some dogs never seem to leave food behind—Labrador Retrievers come to mind—other dogs cache their leftovers for later, burying them in a safe place in the backyard, for example. Dogs often hide their treasures—food or other items of personal importance to them—beneath the earth, then dig them up later to enjoy, if they can remember where they left them.

Cats also may bury their food, but the action serves another purpose altogether. For certain felines, snubbing the food bowl isn't enough to make their point. They'll cover the contents with a page of newspaper or make digging and covering motions with their paws all around the bowl. Cats use this behavior to tell their owners in no uncertain terms what they think of the offered fare.

MORE APPLAUSE FOR CLAWS

Dogs dig for a variety of reasons. Northern breeds used the skill as a survival tool in the Arctic, burrowing deep to keep warm in the iciest weather. Dogs in warm climates dig holes in moist earth during hot weather seeking a cool resting place. My grandmother's dog, Sandy, scooped out dozens of nests in the loose dirt beneath the front porch of the Kentucky farmhouse. It was cool there during the summer, and the porch provided dry shelter in the winter.

Dogs also dig to get where they want to go; they often tunnel beneath fences meant to contain them. Terrier breeds in particular are enthusiastic diggers who live for the thrill of kicking up dirt. These dogs will pockmark a yard until it looks like a moonscape, or they'll help owners plow the garden, whether help is required or not, with their joyful excavations. When confined indoors, these same dogs may empty the soil from the potted palm or the cat's litter box—or even try to tunnel through the carpeting. They come by the urge naturally; the word "terrier" means "of the earth," and these breeds were developed to follow prey into their deep burrows and dig them out.

Some dogs learn to vault fences by using a combination of leaping and pseudo-climbing. Dogs are not built for climbing, but the smarter the dog, the more likely he is to find a way to do what he wants. German Shepherds are notorious climbers; they typically find a corner of a fence and brace themselves on either side as they go up and over. Smaller dogs can also manage high fences. Most dogs, though, have their claws firmly planted on, and in, the ground.

Feline claws aren't used for digging, but serve as grappling hooks for climbing trees and other elevated perches, in addition to clutching prey. The ability to climb serves a couple of functions for the cat. Negotiating higher elevations gives the cat a wider range of prey. Tree-dwelling animals like squirrels and bird babies are easy pickings for the cat who is able to climb to the source. Also, cats hate the unexpected, and high lookouts enable them to keep an eye on what's happening in their world. They will even use an elevated perch as a launching pad for ambushes.

One of the biggest benefits of climbing, though, is protection. Cats often climb to escape a doggy pursuer. That leaves the ground-bound canine barking helplessly below. Cats are quick to use their climbing ability against dogs. The location of the cat's shoulder blades on her sides rather than on her back gives her front legs the wide range of motion that makes tree-hugging possible. Where dogs and cats share the same turf, the cat often will tease Poochie by lounging just out of reach.

The cat can run up a tree as fast as she can run on the ground; however, the curve of the claws makes it easier for Kitty to go up than down, which is why cats often call for help once they've reached the treetops. It's not that they can't come down under their own power, but it's uncomfortable and scary—not to mention undignified—to back down tail first and not see where they're going. They'd rather meow for human help.

JUMPING ON BALANCE

Almost all dogs and cats are phenomenal jumpers. The exceptions are short-legged breeds like the Dachshund and the new-fangled Munchkin cat, but even these and other small breeds get around extremely well. Given their height, even toy and miniature varieties are good jumpers, and the dog of average size is able to leap a very high fence and escape from his yard, as many frustrated owners soon discover. Indoor cats often relish lolling on top of the refrigerator or in some even higher spot.

Cats are incredible leapers, able to jump five times their height from a standing start. This comes in handy when they want to escape the dog's cold nose, and they can turn the tables on a dog by using an elevated perch to stage an ambush.

Nature equipped the tree-climbing cat with a defense mechanism no other animal has to such a degree—the feline sense of balance. The cat's long tail acts as a counterweight that helps her walk high, narrow pathways with ease, even at great speeds.

Should she take a wrong step, her flexibility, vision, agility, and sense of balance will combine to allow her to land on her feet.

MARKING BEHAVIOR

Both cats and dogs indulge in marking behavior, like scratching or urinating on objects, which is thought to serve primarily to identify their territory. They use both scent signals and visual signs. Typically, this behavior is most conspicuous in the intact animal—the sexually potent cat or dog that is still able to produce offspring.

Body waste is a common marking tool of both dogs and cats. In the wild, wolves use urine and feces to mark the boundaries of their territory. Dogs typically are reluctant to defecate when confined on a leash or when an owner is watching, but they don't appear to respond to feces as a signpost the way wolves do. Experts believe domestication has reduced this type of dominance display in dogs. Instead, domesticated dogs almost exclusively use urine to mark their territorial boundaries.

The most obvious example of marking in dogs is the leg-cocking behavior. This pose aims urine at usually vertical objects, leaving a scented signpost at a convenient sniffing height. Urine marking has great social and sexual significance, and male dogs typically indulge in leg-cocking behavior more frequently and readily than females. However, girl dogs also scent-mark either by leg-cocking or squatting to leave their scented urine, particularly when they are advertising their breeding availability to canine Romeos.

Very small amounts of urine do the job. In fact, some dogs may leg-cock with nothing to show for it. These instances usually occur when another dog is present. In effect, the dog that poses but doesn't produce may simply be going through the motions as a visual signal to watching dogs. When emptying a full bladder, females usually urinate in a squatting position, and males occasionally do so as well. Neutering the dog usually reduces urine-marking exuberance, so that bedroom walls, tires, and furniture are less often baptized.

Most people who keep cats are grateful that Kitty uses a litter box and buries her waste. This behavior is thought to be a carryover from her previous existence in the wild where it was used as a protective mechanism. Hiding the waste helped keep the cat's presence hidden, a definite advantage when Kitty had babies to protect. In the wild, however, adult cats are rarely preyed upon, have few natural enemies, and usually hold one of the highest levels in the food chain.

Like wolves, adult cats—both wild ones and our lap kitties—also use urine and feces to mark their territory. Leaving the droppings uncovered is, in wildcats, a sign of dominance and probably marks the territory as occupied. Strange cats crossing a dominant cat's territory see the uncovered waste as an advertisement of ownership. They may bury their own waste when in another's territory to avoid ownership disputes.

Spraying urine is a normal behavior of sexually active cats, especially males. Just as dogs cock their legs, cats back up to the target object and spray onto usually vertical surfaces. When interested only in emptying a full bladder, the cat more typically squats and urinates downward. Neutering drastically reduces a cat's urge to spray urine, preventing household furnishings from being ruined.

Many male dogs and a few females scratch the ground after eliminating, but they don't bury their waste. This dirt-kicking behavior isn't completely understood, but several theories have been suggested to explain it. Scratching or kicking the ground following urination or defecation may help spread the scent; however, dogs may walk away after splashing urine on the side of a building, and kick up grass somewhere else. Some experts believe that a scent may be left behind during the scratching or kicking behavior from glands in the feet and between the toes. Also, the disturbed ground may be a visual sign of territorial marking.

Cats use scratching as a way to mark territory to a much greater degree than dogs. The cat's claws leave both visible signs and scent cues from the glands in the footpads. But where dogs limit their scratching to an outdoor site near their recent elimination, cats want the world to see their signposts. The target is often a vertical object like a tree or fence post, but sometimes cats prefer a horizontal surface they can stretch out upon.

Cats may use hard objects like wood for claw care, but they prefer softer, shredable material for marking. The more marks Kitty can make, the better she likes it. Household furniture is a common target.

Just as chewing feels good and natural to dogs, scratching is a normal behavior for cats; it cannot—and should not—be thwarted. Commercial scratching objects are available to give the cat plentiful and acceptable scratching opportunities.

Cats also mark territory in a way dogs do not. Using special glands found on the face and body, cats rub against objects and leave behind their signature odor. People normally associate this head-rubbing behavior, called bunting, with feline affection; in fact, it is a way for the cat to cover the object with a familiar scent and identify it as a part of her territory. Cats therefore rub against the people on whom they feel they have some claim. They'll also indulge in bunting behavior with friendly dogs. It is a way for animals to reinforce a friendly relationship by sharing scent.

CHAPTER SIX

Canine Courtship and Feline Ardor

Sexual behavior is quite different in cats and dogs. The way that dogs and cats behave toward each other is programmed almost from the moment of birth. Puppies and kittens learn their lessons early, with Mom as their teacher.

Dogs and cats should never be allowed to breed at will, however. Allowing them to do what comes naturally would negate the centuries of work that went into developing the specific breeds we recognize today. Only a select few people who have the appropriate expertise, knowledge, and financial means (yes, it's expensive!) should consider breeding cats or dogs.

This chapter will not tell you how to breed your cat or dog; to do that, you need specific information on genetics, timing, and other details purposely left out of this text. The following is instead a frank discussion of canine and feline sexual physiology and behavior, domestication's influence on pet sexuality, and puppy and kitten development. Understanding these aspects of your pets provides the best argument for neutering, by cataloguing the reasons why intact cats and dogs are so difficult to integrate into a peaceable kingdom.

Nature probably never intended for dogs and cats to be quite the sexual creatures they are. The domestication process has caused profound changes in dog and cat reproduction; through careful selection, we have created pets that are more promiscuous and fertile than their wild forebears. Sexual status affects our pets' health, the way they behave toward one another, and the way they interact with people.

CHOOSING A MATE

Selective breeding is the process by which animals are mated to produce offspring of a particular type. Dogs and cats are selectively bred to promote those characteristics in their offspring that people find most attractive. That can be a certain coat coloring or pattern, body shape, size, or any number of other traits.

But in order for such controlled breedings to be successful, the prospective four-legged parents must be willing to accept the sexual partner chosen for them. Animals that rejected chosen pairings stood in the way of domestication. For that reason, promiscuity in dogs and cats was a desirable trait and was encouraged.

Promiscuous behavior is in direct contrast to life in the wild, where indiscriminate breeding would be catastrophic. In wolf society, only the most dominant pair in the pack are permitted to breed, while other members of the pack assist in rearing the one litter that's born each year. When times are tough, even that chosen pair may forgo raising a litter. Furthermore, monogamy is the rule among wolves, who show a specific preference for one mate. In its infinite wisdom, nature allows only as many animals to be born as the environment can support.

Sexual Maturity

The process of domestication also promoted earlier sexual maturation. Because pet cats and dogs didn't have to work for their food and had better nutrition available, maturation was accelerated. By breeding animals that had this characteristic, the trait was passed on to and enhanced in their offspring. As a result, today's dogs and cats are able to breed and produce offspring at much earlier ages than their wild cousins.

Female wolves don't become sexually mature until they're nearly two years old, and male wolves aren't ready to sire babies until they're three years old. But some female dogs can produce puppies as early as six months of age while males may sire puppies at ten months of age. Large-breed dogs tend to mature more slowly, and may take eighteen to twenty-four months to become sexually mature.

Most male domestic cats are able to sire kittens by nine months of age, while females typically are sexually mature by six or seven months. However, the onset of a female cat's puberty has a great deal to do with the time of year when she is born, and even her breed. A female cat's first breeding season has been known to occur as early as four months, particularly if she's an Oriental breed like the Siamese, which tend to mature much earlier than other breeds. But other cat breeds like Persians may not experience their first breeding season until they're nearly two years old. To reap the most health benefits, neutering should take place prior to sexual maturity.

Season of Love

Female dogs and cats are said to be "in heat" during the time when they become sexually receptive to the male and when breeding takes place. Technically termed "estrus," the seasonal period of canine and kitty romance is also quite distinctive from that of their wild cousins.

Wolves breed only once a year; the receptive season occurs for only a short period each spring. The number of babies produced depends greatly on the health of the mother wolf and the amount of available food, but wolves commonly have litters of four to six cubs.

Wildcats also have only one breeding season in the spring of each year. The litter size averages two to four kittens. The timing of the breeding and subsequent births aids in survival. Young born during the relatively rich summer months benefit from seasonal warmth and more plentiful prey.

In contrast, high fertility marks both of our domestic pet types. Nearly all dog breeds experience two breeding seasons each year, one about every six months. Some breeds experience even more, while a few (like the Basenji) go into heat only once a year.

The number of puppies produced also varies from breed to breed. Typically, the smaller breed dogs have smaller litters, while large dogs may have eight, ten, or even more puppies from a single breeding. Obviously, Poochie's procreation potential is extraordinary.

But the domestic cat outdoes the dog in the reproductive arena. Unlike her wild relatives, the domestic cat does not have the constraints of weather and food shortages to temper her ardor. Domestic cats can produce two and often three litters of kittens every year. Each litter averages four or five furry babies. And these babies, depending on the time of year they're born, will reach their own sexual maturity during a wide range of times. A female cat's estrus is tied to the seasons; in the Northern Hemisphere it typically runs from February through October. That means if a kitten is born in December, she may go into heat as early as April, but if she's born in July, the kitten may not experience estrus until February, at seven months of age.

The combination of promiscuity and increased fertility encourages new generations of pets to be born as quickly as possible. This was important to domestication, because many animals of certain types could be more easily produced in a relatively short period of time. Today the results of this deadly combination are seen in the ongoing tragedy of pet overpopulation.

Signs of Receptivity

The most obvious signs of sexual receptivity in dogs are physical, while in cats they are behavioral. The sexual behavior of mature cats and dogs is quite distinctive.

Sexual behavior in dogs is seen for the first time in puppyhood. During play, male puppies will often mount their siblings, clasping their forelegs about another puppy's body as though trying to climb on top, then thrusting with their pelvis. This is considered normal play behavior. Adolescent male dogs continue their experimentation, much to the chagrin of owners and sometimes other pets in the household. It's not unusual for a sexually interested young male dog to mount anything from an owner's ankles to chair legs and even the disgruntled family cat.

Male dogs also tend to roam farther afield, seeking their doggy ladyloves, and may attempt and accomplish daring escapes even when responsibly confined. They announce their sexual status with active leg-lifting and may mark anything that doesn't move. Intact male dogs can be quite aggressive and will often fight with other males to establish dominance.

Sexually mature male cats are also quite aggressive and tend to roam miles from home seeking romance. They too use urine to mark territory, both indoors and out. The male cat's urine has a distinctive and pungent odor that humans find quite offensive, and it announces the cat's status as a potent breeding male. Referred to as tomcats, these romantic felines enthusiastically defend their territory from other male cats. Their fights are always loud and often become violent, resulting in injuries to the cats involved.

During estrus, the female dog's ovaries produce the hormone estrogen along with a scent that attracts male dogs. The hormone also increases the female's activity and may result in the dog acting more nervous, vocalizing more, and running around to a greater extent.

Estrus lasts approximately twenty-one days in the female dog and is divided into three phases. The onset, called proestrus, lasts six to nine days and is characterized by a swelling of the vulva and a dark bloody discharge. Ovulation, the release of the eggs, occurs during the next phase, which lasts six to twelve days. Once the eggs are released, they must mature in the female for seventy-two hours before they can be fertilized by sperm. The vaginal discharge lightens to a faint pink during "standing heat," the receptive period during which the female will accept the male dog and breeding can take place.

Feline estrus varies in duration, but the receptive period during which Kitty will accept the male's advances usually lasts five to eight days. If she does not become pregnant during this time, there is a resting period of three to fourteen days. Then she goes back into heat. In the Northern Hemisphere, female cats that don't become pregnant will continuously cycle in and out of heat from February through October.

Unlike dogs, female cats don't exhibit obvious physical signs of receptivity. Instead, the cat shows her readiness with obvious, usually obnoxious, behavior signals. Kitty acts exceedingly affectionate toward people and other animals, rubbing against them and seeking attention. During full estrus, she cries and meows, calling out her willingness and desire for a mate. This caterwauling may go on for minutes at a time and may be mistaken for cries of anguish. At the same time, Kitty rolls about on the floor. She often spends a good deal of time with her bottom in the air and her tail held to one side, in a clear gesture of invitation for male cats.

In dogs and cats, neutering prior to sexual maturity drastically reduces—and in many cases eliminates—these obnoxious behaviors. Otherwise, owners may often end up with unwanted litters despite their best intentions.

The Tie that Binds

The scent of the female dog or cat signals the male that she is ready to mate. In both species, the preliminaries include a great deal of exploratory sniffing of the anal regions, but it is ultimately the female who calls the shots and tells the male when she's ready.

The female dog presents her rear to the male and moves her tail to one side when she's interested. The male mounts her, clasping her with his forelegs while thrusting forward. When insertion of the penis takes place, he treads with his rear legs as the semen is released.

The penis then swells within the female's vagina, and muscles in the vagina constrict, tying the pair together. Often, the male dog will then turn around, lifting one rear leg over the penis after dismounting. The genital tie may last from five to sixty minutes as the mated dogs stand tail to tail; the tie must subside on its own, as trying to separate the pair can injure the male.

Cat Contrasts

The female cat indicates her readiness to mate by crouching in front of her partner and crying in a distinctive way that prompts him to mount. The male cat gently grabs her neck in his teeth, almost mimicking the killing bite used to dispatch prey. Then he straddles her and treads with his rear feet, prompting her to arch her back. She raises her bottom and moves her tail to one side. The tom thrusts until he penetrates her vagina, then immediately ejaculates.

Unlike dogs, female cats do not ovulate until stimulated to do so by the mating act. There are spines on the tom's penis which, when withdrawn from the female's vagina, prompt the release of eggs from the ovaries. Ovulation usually takes place within thirty hours of a breeding.

When the male cat withdraws, the female cries or screams out in reaction and immediately rolls away from him. If he's smart, the tom quickly moves out of her way to avoid being attacked. She then usually rolls, stretches, and cleans her genitals for five to ten minutes after mating.

One breeding between a pair of cats may last from thirty seconds to ten minutes. Subsequent breedings may follow immediately or several hours later, and it's possible for one pair of cats to breed more than twenty times during the receptive period.

All too often, unplanned pet pregnancies occur. When that happens, owners must take responsibility for the results.

MAKING BABIES

Gestation is the time period from conception to birth, during which the babies mature inside the mother. The length of gestation varies somewhat between individual animals and occasionally from breed to breed. But the average time period in both cats and dogs is sixty-three to sixty-five days.

The uterus in both dogs and cats is a Y-shaped organ. Each horn of the uterus contains developing puppies or kittens, and the stem of the Y is the birth canal.

It may be difficult to tell that a dog or cat is pregnant during the early stages. Some dog breeds, especially the larger ones, carry puppies high up beneath their ribs. Cats often have only one or two kittens and don't show much at all. During a specific time period, a veterinarian can palpate, or feel, the pet's abdomen to determine if babies are present.

The first sign of pregnancy occurs when the nipples swell and darken. In cats this happens about two or three weeks after conception. It will take five or six weeks into the pregnancy before the mother cat's tummy begins to thicken noticeably. Depending on the number of babies and the amount of fur present, it can be quite difficult to tell she's with child—er, kitten. A noticeably thickened middle in the dog appears about the same time or a bit later, depending on the breed. As the birth draws near, the prospective mother's breasts develop further. The fur on the breasts and genitals, particularly of longhaired cats and dogs, should be clipped before the birth.

About two weeks before the birth of her kittens, the female cat begins to exhibit nesting behavior. As she looks for just the right place to have her babies, she often explores dark, warm, out-of-the-way locations like the linen closet or the laundry hamper.

Dogs seem to postpone nesting behavior until closer to delivery. About twelve to twenty-four hours before having her puppies, the pregnant dog may dig in the garden or rummage in the closet, rearranging the towels. Professional breeders provide a whelping box for dogs and a kittening box for cats. This encourages the pregnant female to sleep in these areas, so that she will hopefully deliver her furry babies there rather than on Grandmother's handmade quilt.

KITTENING AND WHELPING

Just before the babies are born, the mother's body temperature drops by about two degrees to 98–99°F. This happens eight to twelve hours prior to delivery in dogs, and six hours prior to delivery in cats. It can be easy to miss, but it's a sure sign that labor will soon begin.

During the first stage of labor, the mother pants, may act anxious, and tries to get comfortable in the chosen nest. Some dogs may vomit.

Cats typically will lie down to deliver their kittens. Dogs may also recline, but sometimes they stand or squat. Involuntary uterine contractions increase until one of the uterine horns finally pushes the first puppy or kitten into the body of the uterus. The uterus then pushes the baby out into the world.

At this point, the mother should be bearing down to deliver the kitten or puppy. The water bag that surrounds each furry baby should slowly appear and bulge out from the vulva. Called the placental sac, it looks like a dark gray-green bubble as it emerges. This sac should completely pass from the body within thirty minutes. If the contractions break the bag before birth, a straw-colored liquid may be seen, in which case the newborn should be delivered within a few minutes.

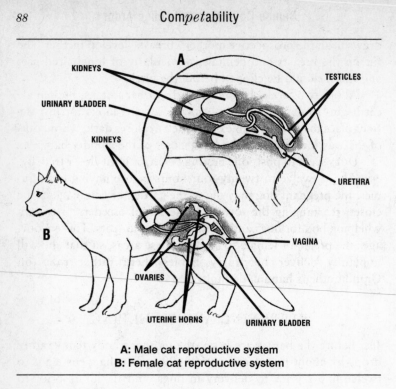

KIDNEYS

URINARY BLADDER

KIDNEYS

B

OVARIES

UTERINE HORNS

A

TESTICLES

URETHRA

VAGINA

URINARY BLADDER

A: Male cat reproductive system
B: Female cat reproductive system

Kittens and puppies may be born either headfirst or in breech position, tail first. Usually the newborn's body is so flexible that a backward presentation isn't a problem. After the first is born, a baby from the other uterine horn begins the journey. The puppies or kittens are expelled from alternating sides of the uterus until all are born.

With either cat or dog mothers, if the baby isn't born after an hour of hard straining, if the mother acts distressed, or if the birth interval is longer than two hours, get the help of a veterinarian.

As each kitten or puppy is born, the mother licks and cleans the newborn and removes the fetal membranes. This not only eliminates any lingering odor, which in the wild might attract a predator to the nest, but also stimulates the baby to breathe and identifies the baby by coating it with the mother's own scent. It also serves to bond the new mother with her litter.

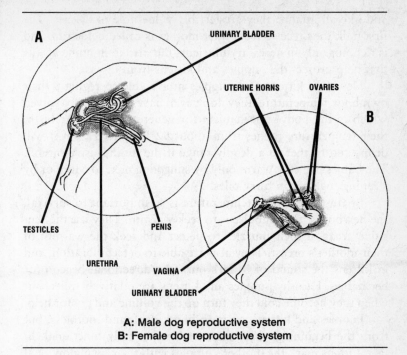

A: Male dog reproductive system
B: Female dog reproductive system

After a kitten or puppy is born, the mother cleans herself and may eat the placenta that accompanies the birth of each baby. She also severs the umbilical cord by biting it. Mothers may nurse the firstborn babies for a while before the next offspring are born.

FURRY NEWBORNS

The new dog or cat mother stays close to her babies for the first day or so, leaving only to use the bathroom or grab a few bites of food. She's much more concerned with her litter than with her own comfort, and she spends most of her time feeding and cleaning them. Newborn puppies and kittens aren't able to eliminate urine or feces without help, so the mother dog or cat licks the babies to stimulate elimination and to keep them clean.

These first few days of nursing are particularly important to the newborns. The babies have no immune system of their own, and like all infants, they are terribly vulnerable to disease. The first milk they receive from their mother is called colostrum and is rich not only in necessary nutrients but also in immune agents that help protect the puppies and kittens from disease.

Newborn kittens and puppies aren't able to regulate their own body temperature; they don't even have the ability to shiver, which is the body's mechanism for generating heat. At birth, their temperature ranges from about 92°F. to 97°F., but it will drop even further to a deadly range if the mother isn't careful. The babies can stay warm only by snuggling next to Mom or by sleeping together in furry piles.

Because the proper temperature is so important to survival, the newborns' first impulse is to seek warmth. They use the sensitive areas of their muzzles to detect and seek the warmth of their mother's breast. They also are able to detect vibration, and in kittens the sound of Mom's purr is a directional beacon for her babies. Healthy puppies and kittens are relatively quiet, but when they become cold they turn up the volume and cry for help.

Puppies and kittens are born blind, deaf, and toothless, but from the beginning, their sense of smell is fully functional. In fact, kittens mark the mother's nipples with their own individual scent and return to the same one each time to nurse.

The babies push against their mother's breasts rhythmically with their forepaws to encourage her milk to flow. Called kneading, this behavior is actually retained into adulthood in the cat and is thought to be a sign of contentment.

The mother cat and dog will continue to nurse the babies for up to eight weeks. The kittens and puppies are kept warm, fed, and protected by their mother during this time. They also learn how to be proper cats and dogs by following her example.

SOCIALIZATION PERIOD

The socialization phase is marked by increased interaction with others. This period begins at about the end of the third week and lasts until about week ten. The critical period, when puppies and kittens form attachments they will carry forward into life, takes place very early in the socialization phase. It is during this period—age six to eight weeks in puppies and two to seven weeks in kittens—that the babies learn who is safe and what is dangerous, and will most easily learn to accept other pets and people as a part of their family. Promoting this pet-people connection is discussed further in Chapter 3.

By three weeks of age, eating and sleeping are no longer the dominating forces in the kitten and puppy existence. Instead, life becomes a game. Everything is new and exciting, and the healthy kitten or puppy displays an unquenchable curiosity. Puppies begin to play with their siblings and tease their mother; similarly, kittens begin to explore their world, wrestle with one another, and attack Mom's tail. During play periods, each learns through hard experience that biting hurts, that claws are sharp, and how best to handle their canine and feline equipment. They also learn to use their teeth without hurting a playmate, and kittens learn how to retract their claws, which, to this point, have been extended all the time.

Birth weight doubles the first week, and by four weeks of age, the babies have again doubled their birth weight. As time goes on, play becomes more and more elaborate. Running, jumping, playing tag, pouncing, and chasing all become part of the repertoire. Playing with novel objects teaches the puppy and kitten what they can and cannot do with that leaf, bug, or string, and helps prepare them for life.

Puppies experience both dominant and subordinate positions during play, which helps prepare them for the social ranking of adult canine life. Play is also a bonding experience; by playing with humans, the puppy or kitten identifies them as safe, fun beings with whom to interact.

It is also during this period that kittens follow Mom to the litter box, watch her scratch in the sand, and quickly begin imitating her bathroom behavior. And they begin grooming themselves. Kittens learn good hygiene from their mother; if Mom is a haphazard groomer or a neatness freak, chances are Junior will follow in her paw steps.

Between four and six weeks of age, the mother's milk production lessens at the same time that puppy and kitten energy needs increase. Though she continues to nurse them for a while, the mother begins leaving the litter alone for longer and longer periods. This reduces the babies' access to her milk.

The mother dog and cat slowly wean their offspring. Hunger coupled with natural curiosity spurs the babies to begin sampling solid food. The new diet will be supplemented with nursing, which may continue for up to eight weeks, but Mom will finally have enough and call it quits. Kittens and puppies are usually completely weaned by eight weeks of age.

It's best for puppies and kittens to delay going to new homes until they're about twelve weeks old. If the babies stay with their littermates and mother for this period, they'll be better adjusted as adults to others of their own species.

JUVENILE PERIOD

The juvenile period begins at around ten weeks of age, when the adolescent cat and dog have an insatiable curiosity about everything, and you must constantly watch them to keep them from getting into trouble. Puppies begin chewing as they teethe, kittens to a lesser extent. While kittens tend to poke their paws and claws into everything, puppies are poking their noses into the same places and often leaving teeth marks behind. While kittens typically have learned to recognize the purpose of the litter box, and do their duty appropriately, puppies must be taught during this time to do the right thing. See Chapter 14 for suggestions on housebreaking.

While the juvenile period may be the most delightful time in a dog or cat's life for everyone else, it's often the most exasperating for the owner. Boundless energy, a short attention span for training and correction, and an ignorance of what's appropriate can conspire to leave your kingdom anything but peaceable.

The juvenile period ends with the onset of sexual maturity, a time in the pet's life that involves special responsibilities for the owner, particularly in terms of the pet's reproductive destiny.

Mankind's interference has made cats and dogs promiscuous and fertile beyond the natural state. Left unchecked, such reproductive excesses can only promote health problems, behavioral disasters, and unwanted progeny destined for the animal shelter and early death.

Responsible owners recognize that caring for a pet includes granting every dog and cat the right to be free of reproductive concerns. The American Veterinary Medical Association currently supports the surgical sterilization of pet dogs and cats as early as four months of age.

The surgery is performed by the veterinarian while the pet is anesthetized and completely asleep. Spaying removes the ovaries and uterus in female pets, while castration (also called neutering) removes the male pet's testicles. The surgery not only prevents accidental breedings but also reduces and in many instances eliminates health problems, like certain cancers, and the roaming, aggression, fighting, urine-marking, and heat behavior typical of sexually intact pets.

When no longer preoccupied with sex, cats and dogs have more time to be pets, enabling you to concentrate on caring for them appropriately.

PART THREE

Bright-Eyed and Bushy-Tailed

CHAPTER SEVEN

Gulp versus Nibble

Thomas speaks proudly of the big bruiser of a cat he had several years ago. Kitty was the boss of the house and reigned supreme over the dog. Kitty even usurped the dog's place at dinnertime, not only eating his own food but chasing away the dog and dining upon kibble as well. He'd crouch over the bowl, crunching with satisfaction while keeping Poochie at bay with an intimidating stare. Thomas speaks of Kitty as a healthy feline, because the cat topped the scales at more than 20 pounds.

Healthy? Not necessarily, in fact, not very likely if the cat habitually ate canine fare. The average female cat weighs 7 to 10 pounds, with a hefty healthy male cat typically weighing 10 to 12 pounds. If a cat is much heavier than that, he's not simply fluffy anymore—he's fat.

But beyond the risk of obesity, there's a very good reason why pet food is labeled for either dogs or cats. Each species requires a very specific diet, and just because pets like to eat from each other's bowls doesn't mean that's good for them. After all, we've all seen some of the things our pets like to put in their mouths.

Simply put, a dog should not eat cat food, and a cat should not eat dog food. It's more than unhealthy—it's downright dangerous. Providing an appropriate balanced diet is probably the single most important thing an owner can do for the health of his pet. If you feed your pet the wrong thing, you risk disease or even death.

DIET BASICS

The most important factor to consider when choosing dog or cat food is the nutrient balance of the food. Nutrients are the parts of food that actually fuel the body. Six different kinds are important for good health: water, fats, carbohydrates, protein, vitamins, and minerals. They work alone and also in combination with one another to provide what the body needs. Just like people, dogs and cats need these nutrients not only in specific amounts but in the right combinations and balance.

Water is the single most important nutrient. The body is able to survive for some time, even weeks, without food, but without water, death will occur within two days.

About 60 percent of the body's volume is composed of water. Water is the principal component of blood and is present both within and around the cells of the body. It helps regulate temperature, lubricates the tissues, and is essential for digestion and elimination. The body loses water through urination, defecation, and exhalation.

Cats and dogs, though, replace lost water in very different ways. When the water ratio in a dog's blood drops to a certain level, the dog is stimulated to drink. To return their water ratio to normal levels dogs tend to drink about twice as much water as they need.

Cats, however, have extraordinarily efficient kidneys and lose much less water through urination than other animals. Cats are generally reluctant to drink; they typically obtain most of their water from the liquid parts of their foods. When fed a canned food diet, Kitty may seldom be found sipping from the water bowl because canned cat foods are up to 83 percent water.

The feline reluctance to drink water can contribute to urinary tract problems and can make it more difficult for ill and dehydrated cats to recover promptly. For instance, a dog would take only about one hour to recoup a 6 percent water deficit, but a cat with the same deficit would need at least twenty-four hours to rehydrate.

Fats are the high-energy component of food. They provide 2¼ times more energy than a comparable amount of carbohydrate or protein. High-fat diets can be beneficial to pets with high energy requirements, such as working dogs and pregnant cats. Fats also help make food taste good, and cats and dogs particularly like animal fats.

Besides energy, fats are the only source for essential fatty acids, or EFAs. These are called essential because they are required by the cat and dog but cannot be manufactured by the body and so must be present in the food. EFAs are necessary for the body to utilize fat-soluble vitamins. Both dogs and cats require the EFAs linoleic acid and linolenic acid; in addition, the cat requires arachidonic acid.

Carbohydrates provide energy and are most commonly derived from cereal grains like corn, wheat, oats, rice, and barley. Carbohydrates also contain dietary fiber, which helps regulate the bowels and assists in the absorption of other nutrients.

Protein provides energy to the cat or dog and is a building block of bone, blood, tissue, and the immune system. We most often think of protein as coming from animal sources—meat and fish. However, cereal grains also provide a good amount of protein, which is why they are often found in great quantities in pet foods. Just as carbohydrates are made up of smaller components like sugars and starches, proteins are built of twenty-three different chemical compounds called amino acids. About half of these amino acids are referred to as essential, because the body can't produce enough of them, so they must be supplied by the diet.

Cats and dogs require the same ten amino acids: histidine, isoleucine, leucine, arginine, methionine, phenylalanine, threonine, tryptophan, valine, and lysine. But unlike dogs, cats also require an eleventh dietary amino acid called taurine. All animals, including humans and dogs, require taurine, but the cat is the only known animal that can't make enough of it to meet its needs. That's why manufacturers supplement cat food with taurine. The cat that doesn't receive sufficient amounts of taurine may go blind or develop fatal heart disease—and this can happen if Kitty eats only dog food.

Cats also require more dietary protein than do dogs. A dog may live quite nicely on a properly balanced vegetarian diet, but a vegetarian diet will kill a cat. However, it's not just the content but also the balance of nutrients that makes the food healthy. An all-meat diet won't provide balanced nutrition, either.

Dogs and cats also require tiny amounts of vitamins and minerals in their diet; these work together in the body at the cellular level. Commercial pet foods are formulated to provide the proper amounts of each. Again, there are differences between cats and dogs. For instance, plant-synthesized beta-carotene must be converted to the actual vitamin A before the body can use it. Dog bodies can do this efficiently, but cats cannot and must rely on the naturally occuring vitamin A found in animal sources like liver and fish oils.

Giving your cat and dog vitamin supplements will not be necessary if they eat a balanced commercial diet; it may actually be dangerous, because supplementation can throw the diet out of balance. Too much can be as bad as too little, however, and can result in deficiencies or toxicities that can cause a wide range of health disturbances, from bone deformities to neurological problems.

DIET DIFFERENCES

It is extremely difficult to formulate balanced diets for our pets, but fortunately the researchers of pet food manufacturers have done the job for us. Just like human food, commercial diets for dogs and cats must comply with national, state, and local regulations that dictate what goes into the food, the way it's distributed, and even how it's labeled. Foods claiming to be complete and balanced must prove those claims in tests developed by the appropriate governing body. This is not as complicated as it sounds. All the pet owner really has to do is look for a statement on the label that says the product has been tested and is in compliance with protocols established by the Association of American Feed Control Officials (AAFCO).

The best foods offer complete and balanced diets that have been substantiated through feeding trials. The label should make the following statement or a similar one: "Animal feeding tests using AAFCO procedures substantiate that [name of product] provides complete and balanced nutrition for [whatever life stage]." If the product doesn't say it's complete and balanced, feed your pet something else.

"Life stage" is the age and sometimes the reproductive status of the pet, and the diets are formulated to best fit those specific times of life. This is important because babies have different energy requirements than do adults. A growing puppy or kitten needs two to four times more energy per pound of body weight than does an adult dog or cat.

An adult pet that is fed a growth food will gain weight because the food contains many more calories than the pet needs. Similarly, a kitten or puppy won't grow well when fed on an adult ration. Pet foods are generally labeled either for growth (puppies or kittens), for reproduction (the pregnant or nursing mom), for maintenance (the adult cat or dog), or for all life stages. Beyond these basic categories, there are a host of diets available for the special needs of individual pets, from weight-control to high-performance formulations and even prescription diets for controlling medical conditions. Be sure to pick the right product for your pet.

CANNED OR DRY FOOD

Modern pet food comes in two basic forms: canned and dry. In general, canned foods tend to be extremely tasty, and dogs and cats often eat them quite willingly. However, canned foods may be a bit pricier than the dry products. A great deal of the content is water, which makes the food taste good and may help the cat ingest more water than she would otherwise. But it also dilutes the nutritional content of the food, so that pets need to eat more of a canned diet than a dry diet to fulfill their nutritional needs. Feeding canned food to a large dog becomes expensive very quickly. Canned foods must also be refrigerated after opening, or they will spoil, so they must be fed as meals and not left out all day for free-feeding.

Dry pet foods are the most economical and convenient for the owner. They can be purchased in large quantities and left in the bowl all day without spoiling, and the dog or cat needs to eat less dry food than canned to fulfill its nutritional needs. Dry foods also help prevent dental problems, whereas canned food may stick to the pet's teeth.

The Taste Test

How well a cat or dog likes a particular food will depend on its odor, taste, and texture. Of these, the smell of the food is probably the most important.

Odor is what gets the cat or dog to take that first bite. Pets decide whether or not to eat based on aroma alone, and cats often reject a food before they even taste it.

Humans often select food on the basis of how it looks, however, so pet food manufacturers design foods that will appeal to us because we're the ones who open our pocketbooks. Pets, of course, don't care what the food looks like. They're more interested in the texture: how the food feels in the mouth, how wet or dry it is, and even how the kibble is shaped. Cats hate the feel of dry foods that turn to powder when they're crunched; they relish those that break cleanly. You'll notice all kinds of interesting cat kibble shapes, from stars to O's, and each has been through exhaustive tests to determine which shape has the most mouth appeal.

But dogs tend to be less discriminating than cats and will often swallow anything that doesn't move quicker than the dog.

Most cats and dogs are happy to eat one thing all the time, particularly if they haven't been exposed to an ongoing array of choices. There is a school of thought that believes a pet can actually be taught to be finicky when encouraged to eat a wide variety of tasty foods. In fact, there are animals that for whatever reason demand a change every day and refuse to eat without it. In general, dogs take about three weeks for a diet change to become ingrained. Cats don't take as long, perhaps only a day or two. Between individual pets, there's a great deal of disparity.

Do dogs and cats need variety in their diet? No. And if variety is never offered, they'll never miss it. You'll make your life much simpler, and keep your pets healthier and less stressed, if you feed them the same sound diet from day one.

Canine Gluttons

The way you feed your dog and cat can be as important as what you feed them. And no, it's not always as simple as plopping something into a bowl. When dogs and cats are left to their own devices, their natural tendencies can get them into trouble.

The eating styles of dogs and cats are distinctly different, and have their root in the pets' body structures. The overall size difference, the claws-or-teeth method of capturing and holding prey, dental differences, and even a different gustatory sense all have an impact on the way each pet prefers to dine.

There are exceptions to every rule, and all dogs and cats are individuals with their own idiosyncrasies. But it's safe to say that most dogs tend to be gluttons. They came by this tendency honestly. Ancestors of the dog hunted in packs, enabling them to kill large prey animals, which supplied them with massive amounts of food. But it wasn't as if the pack could put leftovers in the deep freeze for later. Other animals were waiting in the wings to steal, or at least nibble and scavenge, the remains. Anything the wolf-dogs didn't eat in one meal was up for grabs; the rule was use it or lose it.

Consequently, the ancestors of our modern dogs became highly talented gorgers able to handle huge amounts of food at one time. After stuffing themselves to overflowing, the pack would settle down to digest the feast, sometimes for days at a time. They didn't need to hunt as often, because each meal lasted them for days rather than hours.

Think about it—where do you think the term "wolfing down food" came from? There's a report of a wolf that went without food for seven days, then ate one-fifth of its body weight in one meal. That's like a 180-pound man polishing off a 36-pound steak.

Many modern dogs, particularly hound-type dogs, have retained this ability. They don't chew; they simply grab mouthfuls of food, swallow, and keep eating until the bowl is empty. Beagles and Labradors are notorious gorgers.

In addition, dogs have a sweet tooth, just like people. It makes perfect sense—fruits and vegetables that are richest in calories are also the sweetest, and that's why we choose to eat them.

Dogs possess a number of flat molars, designed specifically for mashing and grinding vegetable matter. Wolves often eat grass and ripe berries, while foxes are said to relish grapes and sweet corn, and our domestic dogs are no different. This ability and willingness to eat a variety of foods is what made wolves such adaptable survivors. It's no wonder that many dogs plant themselves under the dinner table and inhale anything, from fruit to fish, that falls within snapping distance.

The dog's enthusiasm for food, though, can be problematic if Poochie shares dinnertime and space with a cat. That's because cats tend not to finish a meal in one sitting, but often leave food in the bowl for later.

Finicky Felines

While dogs lean toward gluttony, cats are at the other end of the spectrum. Felines have a reputation for being finicky eaters, but actually they're just more discriminating than dogs about what, and how much, they eat.

Remember, cats are the archetypical carnivore. Kitty doesn't have the dog's flattened molars because she doesn't eat fruit and vegetables. And because she eats only animals, she has no need to detect sweet flavors.

The forebears of domestic cats typically hunted small prey like mice, rabbits, rats, and sometimes insects. These were bite-size morsels, generally swallowed whole, and one little mouse probably didn't go very far. Therefore, small cats needed to kill three or four times a day to satisfy their hunger. The way domestic cats feed is a reflection of this evolutionary pattern. Cats are nibblers rather than gorgers like dogs. Left to their own devices, cats eat small mouse-size portions several times a day. Owners who are used to the gulping behavior of dogs may think Kitty is snubbing the bowl if she leaves food behind, when actually three or four bites may satisfy her immediate craving. She'll come back for more throughout the day.

Cats also quickly learn to avoid eating certain foods. Studies have shown that when cats are fed a diet that's deficient in thiamin, they will refuse to eat that food after a few days. In fact, the thiamin deficiency causes a feeling of malaise, which the cat probably associates with the type or flavor of the food, causing her to avoid that food in the future. This aversion to certain foods evolved as a way for the wild feline to avoid toxins and insufficiencies in their diet. In one study, the cats learned after only one meal to avoid a diet that made them feel bad, and they remembered that aversion up to eighty days later.

This built-in mechanism could be misinterpreted by pet cats in some circumstances. For instance, the cat suffering a bout of diarrhea due to intestinal worms could associate the illness with its most recent meal and so avoid foods of that flavor in the future. This may be the reason that Kitty suddenly refuses a diet that she accepted in the past.

Domestication seems to have tempered or even eliminated this response in our pet dogs. It's not unusual for the pet dog to become ill, lose his lunch, and then eat the vomitus.

Suppertime!

Dogs and cats have very strong opinions about when they want to be fed. Usually it's right now! Instant gratification is not always possible, however, nor is it the healthiest choice for the pet.

Wild animals have very little to say about when they'll eat; they're at the mercy of opportunity. That's probably why cats don't have to be hungry to hunt. In the wild, the hunting reflex can't be coupled with hunger, or opportunities would be missed.

Pet dogs and cats don't have to depend on happenstance; they are offered nutritious, balanced meals in adequate quantities. How often, then, should the dog or cat be fed?

The differences in their feeding habits along with the way their bodies process food will determine how often the cat and dog should be fed. The timetable will vary with individuals as well, but some general rules can be followed.

First, let's compare how long food stays in the body of each. About twenty-four hours will elapse from the time a dog swallows food to the time that food is processed. This same sequence takes only thirteen hours in the cat. (In people it can take up to fifty-six hours.)

Cats tend to do very well with free-feeding—that is, when food is placed in a bowl and the cat has access to it all hours of the day. This way the feline nibbler is able to indulge whenever she feels the urge, and she will typically consume anywhere from eight to twenty-four small meals spread throughout the twenty-four-hour period.

Some dogs, particularly miniature breeds, do equally well with free feeding. But where cats nibble twenty-four hours a day, dogs typically shut down their appetite at night when they go to bed and rev it up when the family wakes up the next morning. This probably has something to do with the dog's sociability. Perhaps he doesn't want to eat alone but considers mealtime a social event to be enjoyed in a group, when his people are up and about.

Doggy gorgers must be fed only at mealtime to keep their weight from ballooning. For adult dogs, a once-daily regimen often works well. Both dogs and cats can adjust to multiple feedings throughout the day, but cats don't do well on once-daily meals. They seem unwilling or unable to eat enough at one sitting to carry them through the whole day. Cats do quite well on twice-daily feedings, though. Unlike dogs, cats seem able to adjust their food intake so that they consume just the right number of calories to maintain their weight, whether they have two meals or twenty-four throughout the day.

The effects of social structure on feeding habits pose another complication for the multi-pet household (this is discussed in greater detail in Chapter 12). Dogs are group-oriented pets that prefer to feed with the pack, which inevitably leads to competition for the choicest portions. In fact, many dogs tend to eat more when they perceive mealtime as a competition—a kind of "I'll eat it so he won't get it" mentality.

Cats, on the other paw, hunt by themselves and typically eat alone. Because they tend to eat smaller amounts all day long—particularly if they know the food is out all the time—they don't get nearly as competitive over the food as dogs do.

Feeding Strategies

Before planning your pets' mealtime, examine your situation. Is your dog a glutton who inhales everything in sight? Or is he a dainty eater, able to feed responsibly from a never-empty bowl? The way your dog eats is, to a certain extent, going to determine the way you feed the cat.

It goes without saying that both pets must have their own food and water bowls. They are best fed on opposite ends of the room; sometimes separate rooms are required.

You'll want to schedule your pets' mealtimes at your convenience, not theirs. If your dog is a sensible eater and can be free-fed, thank your lucky stars! You'll be able to put down canine kibble in one corner, and kitty kibble in the other, and allow the pair to munch as they will. But if your dog is a gorger, he'll finish his own food, then head for the cat's bowl. Free-feeding the cat can provide a never-ending banquet for the dog. Some cats may step aside and let Poochie eat his fill. Others will throw a hissy fit. Neither scenario is good.

The canine glutton must be meal-fed. When the dog has the run of the house, free-feeding Kitty is very difficult. The simplest solution is to meal-feed the cat as well. And since Kitty does much better on two meals, have the dog dine twice as well. Feed them at the same time, in the morning and evening, on opposite sides of the kitchen or in separate rooms. Wait until both are finished before allowing them to leave the bowl. Allow your dog fifteen to twenty minutes to eat, then pick up his food whether he's finished eating or not. Most gorgers will inhale the food very quickly, and dogs learn to eat in a time frame when they know food will be taken away. Give cats a bit more time, say thirty minutes or even longer, when the food isn't accessible to the dog. Cats generally appreciate a quiet place in which to dine, so sequestering Kitty's meals in the laundry room probably won't put her whiskers in a twist.

Food is near and dear to the hearts of all cats and dogs. And satisfying our pets' hunger goes a long way toward promoting good health and keeping the peace.

❦

CHAPTER EIGHT

Hairballs and Hot Spots

Whether long, short, curly or silky, shaggy or smooth, your pet's fur covering is one of the most noticeable things about him. More than an attractive covering, skin and coat condition are a mirror of your pet's health. All cats and dogs benefit from regular skin and coat care. In many cases, it's up to the owner to help the pet look good.

Much depends on the pet's coat type, which varies from breed to breed. And individual animals may be quite fastidious, or slovenly little pigs. Not all dogs need regular bathing, while some cats require it.

In addition to caring for their fur, a good groomer pays attention to eyes, ears, claws, and teeth. There are differences in grooming-related problems between dogs and cats. Owners of both species may experience canine hot spots and/or feline hairballs at least once, along with the bane of pets and owners alike, fleas. Be warned, though, that flea treatments affect cats and dogs very differently.

THE NEATNIKS

Cats have a well-deserved reputation as meticulous groomers. Felines take a great deal more responsibility for their appearance than dogs do. Cats keep their fur in shape by licking themselves, using their rough tongue and nibbling teeth as a kind of kitty comb. A cat will tongue-dampen her paw and use it as a wash-cloth, which she rubs over her face and head in places that she can't reach with her tongue. She uses her rear claws to comb her fur, particularly at the back of her head and ears. Grooming waterproofs the cat's coat by spreading skin oils over the fur. It also helps to remove parasites like fleas.

Mother cats groom their babies, and kittens learn the behavior by mimicking Mom. They begin licking themselves by two weeks of age.

Sometimes adult cats groom each other, particularly in hard-to-reach places like the back of the neck. In homes with both dogs and cats, Kitty often grooms the dog, too. This is more of a social behavior than one of cleanliness, though, and can be a sign of affection between pets.

FELINE HAIRBALLS

Adult cats spend up to 50 percent of their awake time grooming themselves. By licking herself, the cat removes loose dead fur that might otherwise form painful knots.

The cat swallows the hair that sticks to her tongue during grooming. It typically passes through the digestive tract and is deposited in the litter box. But if swallowed hair is not passed, it collects in the stomach and is compressed into a wad of fur, which can be expelled only by vomiting. The dense hot dog–shaped masses that she spits up are called hairballs. Barefoot owners sometimes step on these noxious offerings in the middle of the night.

Vomiting an occasional hairball is a perfectly normal occurrence for most cats, but if the wad of hair becomes too massive, it can become impossible to expel by vomiting or defecating and can block the intestinal tract. Signs of a problem hairball are constipation, diarrhea, loss of appetite, or retching without results. If the digestive tract becomes completely blocked—one sign of this is frequent vomiting—the result can be deadly, and the problem may require surgery.

Commercial hairball remedies are available, which usually contain a nondigestible fat-type ingredient. These products work by slicking down the mass of fur and lubricating the gut so the hairball passes more easily. Take care not to overuse hairball remedies, though, because excessive amounts can interfere with the cat's ability to metabolize vitamins. Ask your veterinarian to recommend a product.

Home remedies may be as effective as commercial preparations. Many cats seem to relish unmedicated petroleum jelly. If you occasionally dab some on your cat's paw, she'll willingly lick it off like a treat. Extra fiber in the diet can also help move the hairball through the intestines. Try a high-fiber diet or add a fiber supplement to her food. A spoonful of canned pumpkin will work, as will plain bran or unflavored Metamucil.

Before you try a commercial or home remedy for hairballs, though, try something much simpler. You can reduce or even eliminate most hairball problems by combing or brushing your cat regularly. Any loose fur you're able to remove by grooming, the cat won't swallow.

CANINE HOT SPOTS

Dogs do attend to some aspects of self-grooming. They use their rear claws to scratch themselves, their teeth to nibble burrs or dirt from their fur, and their tongue to clean the genital regions. Sometimes, though, dogs become overenthusiastic about licking and nibbling themselves. Skin irritation prompts the dog to scratch or lick the spot. The result can be a bacterial skin infection, commonly referred to as a hot spot.

A hot spot is a circular area of hair loss and skin infection that appears without warning and spreads very quickly. The typically swollen, warm, weepy sore can grow to several inches in diameter within a few hours. The infection often smells bad and secretes pus.

Hot spots can appear nearly anywhere on the body; the back, flanks, rump, and tail are common sites. Dog breeds that have heavy double coats seem most prone to developing hot spots immediately prior to shedding, when dead hair may be trapped next to the skin.

A hot spot is treated primarily by getting air to the infection and preventing the dog from continually biting at it. A restraint called an Elizabethan collar may be secured around the dog's neck to prevent him from licking or nibbling the wound.

Hot spots are often extremely painful, and a veterinarian must sedate the dog before treatment can begin. The vet then clips away the hair surrounding the area, cleanses the skin with an antibacterial preparation like diluted hydrogen peroxide, and then applies a medication to the area. Sulphadene, available at most pet stores, seems to work quite well to dry the sore. The veterinarian may prescribe an ointment to reduce the irritation, and sometimes antibiotic pills are required to clear up the infection. Ultimately, the underlying problem—fleas, allergy, or whatever—must be addressed.

Since dogs don't groom themselves as religiously or as well as cats, owners must take full responsibility for canine coat care. Grooming during shedding season is particularly important and can help prevent hot spots from developing.

ROUTINE COAT CARE

There are five basic coat types, each requiring slightly different care. Breeds with *long hair and an undercoat* include Collies and German Shepherds, and the Persian and Himalayan cats. These dogs can get by with a thorough weekly combing and brushing, but the cat breeds need daily attention.

Non-shedding curly-coated breeds include Poodles and Bedlington Terriers; their fur grows constantly and must be clipped about every two months. Rex cats also have a curly non-shedding coat, but the hair is never clipped.

Silky-coated breeds include the Afghan Hound, Lhasa Apso, Maltese, Pekingese, and all of the setters and spaniels. These dogs require regular and consistent combing and brushing to prevent matting; weekly is good but daily is better. Cats in this category are the Turkish Angora and Turkish Van.

Smooth-coated breeds include the Boxer, Dachshund, Rottweiler, and Greyhound, and the Bombay, Siamese, and other shorthaired cats. Medium-length smooth coats are maintained with a comb and a bristle brush; very short coats require only a curry brush or a chamois. You can also slip an old pair of panty hose over your hand and stroke the smooth-coated dog or cat with that. It works as well as expensive grooming equipment to polish the fur.

Wiry-coated dog breeds include most terriers and the Schnauzer; there's only one wire-coated cat breed, appropriately named the American Wirehair. Comb these coats at least once a week. These dogs also require specialized plucking equipment that removes the dead hair from a tight wiry coat, and this should be done about four times a year. A groomer can perform clipping and plucking service for your dog as needed.

Large dogs can be groomed on the ground or the floor as you kneel beside them; medium to small pets, especially toy dogs and cats, should be placed on a table at waist level, which helps confine their movements. Some pets do better when one person lightly restrains them while the other does the combing and brushing; others go into ecstasy when groomed and will beg you not to stop.

Pet brushes and combs are available in a wide variety, along with many specialty items for specific breeds. Show-grooming for dogs can include poofing and trimming the hair into extravagant bouffant styles, and a professional groomer or breed expert can best show you how to trim a curly- or woolly-coated dog like the Poodle. But all owners should learn how to keep their pets' coat clean, and prevent painful mats.

A rubber curry brush works well on shorthaired pets, while a slicker brush, which has fine wire bristles embedded in a rubber pad, is more appropriate for thicker, longer hair. The pin-and-bristle brush has metal pins on one side for removing loose hair, and natural bristles on the other for smoothing the coat. Teflon-coated combs don't pull or break the fur and reduce the level of static electricity. Choose the widest-toothed comb for dressing long, thick fur; the finest combs work well on smooth-coated shorthaired cats and dogs. Use a medium-toothed comb on silky-coated and wire-haired pets.

Always comb or brush in the direction the fur grows, and begin with light, short strokes. When grooming thick, long fur, comb the surface hair first; then work your way deeper until you're combing clear to the skin. Take care, though, that you don't press too hard; comb gently when you get close to the skin to keep from hurting the pet. Once thoroughly combed, long-coated and thick-furred pets are finished with a brush. Short- to medium-coated pets can start with the brush.

Begin with the sides of the face, the throat, and the neck, then progress down the back and sides. Avoid pressing too hard against the tender backbone and the nipples, and don't neglect the tail. Cats will let you know they like what you're doing by purring or by arching their back into the brush or comb. Dogs often will moan and groan with enjoyment and willingly present their tummy for brushing or combing. Cats tend to resent attention to this area, so while Kitty is still standing, lift one rear leg an inch or so off the table while combing her underside; this puts her a bit off-balance and makes her concentrate on that rather than on what you're doing. It also gives you better access. Remember to groom the genital area and the flanks, inside and out.

When old, dead fur falls out and is caught in long outer hair, painful mats can develop. Mats occur most frequently during the spring and fall shedding seasons, but they can be a year-round problem in some pets, like Persian cats. You'll find problems in the "armpit" regions of all four legs, behind the ears, and beneath the tail. Comb vigilantly to prevent mats from developing.

You can tease a minor mat out with a coarse-toothed comb, starting at the very tip and slowly working deeper. Don't use scissors; you could cut the skin. A badly matted coat may need to be clipped; this should be done by a professional groomer.

Bathing Your Pet

Dogs tend to be bathed more often than necessary, which can strip natural oils from the coat and dry the skin. Cats, on the other hand, tend to be bathed too seldom. Yes, you can give your cat a bath without taking your life in your hands, for sometimes Kitty gets quite grubby, and nothing short of a dunking will do the job.

Plan to bathe German Shepherds and similarly coated dogs only twice a year. The Poodle-type coat, though, will need washing with every trim, about every two months. Silky and wiry coats do well with four baths a year, while the smooth-coated pets may need a bath only once a year, and then only if they get smelly or dingy-looking.

Comb or brush your pet thoroughly before bathing. Water will turn mats to cement and make them impossible to remove without clipping. For medium to large dogs, the bathtub is appropriate, although a garden hose on the patio may work well as long as the day is warm and sunny. For small dogs and cats, a waist-high sink is easier on your knees.

Use only shampoos that have been approved for pets. People products are generally much too harsh and will dry the animal's skin and possibly cause an allergic reaction. Never use dish-washing soap, laundry detergent, or other household cleaners; some may actually poison your pet.

Dogs and cats object to baths when they're frightened. Get ready ahead of time by having towels and pet shampoo already assembled and the tub filled with water before you bring in the pet. It's easier to bathe the pet when both hands are free. Bath tethers are available that can be secured to the porcelain with a suction cup at one end while the other clips to the dog's collar or the cat's harness. Always use a harness on a cat; her fragile neck could be injured by fighting a collar.

Before beginning, place cotton in the pet's ears to keep out the water. You can make your cat more comfortable by placing a secure foothold, like a towel or rubber mat, in the bottom of the tub or sink. A plastic milk crate works well, too, and offers kitty claws something to clutch other than your arm.

Use a plastic cup or ladle to dip water over the pet, or use a hand-held shower spray. Pets, especially cats, may be frightened by the spray, so use it only at a low pressure and keep it close to the coat to soak the fur.

Many pet protests are prompted by water in the face. Don't spray or dunk your pet's face; use a washcloth to clean and rinse this area. Once the fur is wet, apply a thin stream of pet sham-poo along the back, suds your cat or dog thoroughly, then rinse.

For some cats, the dunking method works better. Fill a dou-ble sink, or a pair of buckets set in the bathtub, with warm water. Gently lower the cat into the water, letting him clutch the side with his front paws so he's standing on his hind legs. Lift him out once he's wet (don't splash his face), and soap him while he drips onto a towel. Then lower him back into the container to rinse; lift him out and give him a second rinse in the clean water in the other container.

The most important part of giving a dog or cat a bath is getting all the soap off afterward. When you're absolutely sure the shampoo is gone, rinse the pet once more for good measure before calling it quits. For dogs especially, be prepared to get your own shower when they shake off after their bath. Don't forget to remove the cotton from the ears. Shorthaired pets will air-dry before too long, but those with more fur will need lots of towels and sometimes a blow-dryer on a low setting.

Flea Treatment

Fleas, blood-sucking insects that live on a pet's skin, are the most common parasite of dogs and cats. Fleas tend to be more common during warm summer months, but they can infest the house and afflict indoor pets year-round. In addition to causing itchy irritation, fleas spread disease and health problems, including anemia, allergy, and tapeworm (this is discussed further in Chapter 11).

Most often fleas are easily detected, since you can see them on the pet, though cats tend to groom away most of their fleas. Other indications of flea infestation include a pepperlike residue of flea dirt on the pet's skin, particularly at the root of the tail. Evidence of tapeworm—ricelike debris caught in the fur near the pet's tail or in the stool—is a sure sign fleas are present, because most pets get this intestinal parasite when they swallow an infected flea.

Fleas typically live about thirty days, and during that time the female flea can lay fifty eggs a day. The flea matures from egg to larva, spins a cocoon, then emerges as an adult. Though adult fleas reside primarily on the pet, they can be found in their other life stages in the yard and the house. To eradicate the bugs, both the pet and the environment must be treated.

Many flea products are available to protect cats and dogs from these biting pests. Be aware, though, that insecticides are toxic substances designed to kill, and that cats are extremely sensitive to many of the chemical substances traditionally used to kill fleas. When used on dogs, these products may work well. A dog product used on a cat, however, may kill not only the fleas but the cat as well. Before you use any product on your cat or dog, be certain you understand all the directions, and follow them carefully.

There are better methods of flea control than bathing. The newer products are safer and more effective than many of the old standbys like collars, dips, and powders. The best ones use compounds that repel, sterilize, or kill the flea without endangering the dog or cat.

Imadacloprid (Advantage) kills adult fleas, and fipronil (Frontline Top Spot) kills both adult fleas and ticks. These products are applied as drops to the pet's skin on a monthly basis. They are currently available only through veterinarians.

Claw and Nail Care

Dog toenails and cat claws are composed of the same hard substance, but their function differs. Normal canine wear and tear and feline scratching don't always accomplish the whole job of

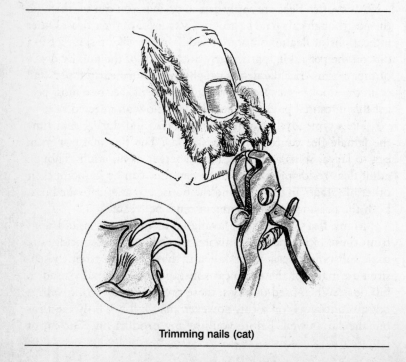

Trimming nails (cat)

maintaining the claws. Overgrown nails tend to curl and become caught in bedding and carpets, and they may split or tear. Keeping the toenails trimmed to a manageable length is healthier for the pet and helps reduce inappropriate scratching and digging.

With cats, a monthly trim is usually sufficient. Active outdoor dogs may not need frequent nail trimming, but indoor dogs often require a monthly trim. Dewclaws on the inside of the lower leg require particular attention.

Of all grooming care, nail trimming is perhaps the most universally despised by owners and pets alike. Trimming the nails too short will "quick" them—cut into the living vessel that feeds the nail bed and cause them to bleed. This is uncomfortable for the pet and disconcerting for the owner, but it's not easy to avoid when the cat or dog refuses to hold still.

Unless your cat or dog is nearly comatose, or extremely well trained, get help. I was able to trim my Fafnir's nails by myself, but only because the German Shepherd had been trained to be a gentleman. It's best to have one person trim the nails and another person hold the pet so he won't wiggle and injure himself.

Always use the right tool for the job. A variety of pet nail trimmers can be found, from scissor action to guillotine type. For tiny cat claws, human nail or toenail clippers may be all you need to snip off the points. The clippers you choose must be sharp, and you must be comfortable using them. A dull tool will crush or split the nail, and if you're not confident wielding the clippers, why should your pet trust you?

Take your time—there's no law that says you must trim every nail on every paw at one sitting, nor is it written that you must lop a quarter inch off the nail. If your pet's claws are clear or white, the pink quick, the living nail bed, will be visible, so you can avoid the danger zone. But many dogs have dark, opaque nails that leave you guessing. Take off less rather than more—clip off only the tips of the nails. This is particularly important if they have been allowed to grow long, because the quick will have grown longer, too. Tipping will prompt the quick to draw back into the nail bed. If you tip the nails once a week, they should be in good shape by the end of the month. And if you don't quick the claw, your pet will be much more willing to endure the exercise the next time around.

It's best to expose the cat and dog to nail trimming while they're still babies. Pets are easier to handle at that size, and they'll learn that there is life after a nail trim.

There are several restraint techniques that work well. With medium to large dogs, kneel on the floor next to the reclining pet. Place one arm under, up, and around the dog's neck, and snug Poochie's head to your chest, while the other arm goes over the dog's back and down across his side, pulling his body close.

Place small dogs and cats on a waist-high table, lay them on their side, and rest your forearm on their shoulder and neck with gentle, firm pressure while that hand captures both forelegs. Rest your other forearm across the pet's hips with your hand grasping the rear legs.

It goes without saying that the pet should be familiar with and trust the restrainer, and that person should speak soothingly to the pet during the entire procedure. Some cats may do better without any restraint, though, particularly those who resent being held more than they fear the nail trimming itself.

Dog nails are clearly visible, but be careful not to catch any hair in the trimmers; this can be as uncomfortable as quicking. Cat claws, on the other hand, must be manipulated in order to appear. Gently grasp the paw and press between your fingers, and the claws will appear. Cats will file down any sharp edges left by the trimming during their next round with the scratching post, but dog nails need to be filed after trimming. Use an emery board, or buy a suitable nail file at a pet supply store.

Should you quick the nail despite your precautions, use a styptic pencil to stop the bleeding. With cats and small dogs, raking the claw through a bar of soap will also work.

If the cat or dog becomes very agitated before you've finished, call it a day and finish later. Offer a special reward to your pet—a treat, or a favorite game—to let him associate pleasant things with nail trimming.

Ear Maintenance

The amount of ear care required varies from pet to pet. Healthy ears are pink, have no discharge, and require only basic mainte-

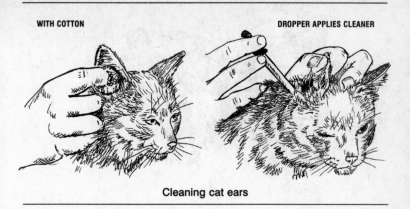

WITH COTTON   DROPPER APPLIES CLEANER

Cleaning cat ears

nance about once a month. A small amount of amber ear wax is normal and helps protect the ear canal.

Commercial ear-cleaning solutions are available from veterinarians and pet stores, but a bit of mineral oil, baby oil, or diluted hydrogen peroxide is fine for general cleaning. Never drip cleaner—or anything else, for that matter—down into the ear canal unless you're instructed to do so by your veterinarian.

Instead, place a few drops of the cleaner on a cotton ball or soft cloth, grasp the ear flap firmly with one hand, and gently swab out the visible portion of the external ear with the other. You can use a cotton swab to clean out the whorls and indentations in the ear flap, but don't push down into the canal itself. That can pack debris into the ear and risk damage to the hearing mechanism. Remember to wear old clothes; after cleaning, the pet will shake his head and fling excess cleaning solution on anything in his path.

Pets that have floppy ears, like Cocker Spaniels, or folded-over ears, like the Scottish Fold cat, require more attention than pets with erect ears. Trapped moisture and poor air circulation provide a perfect environment for ear infections.

Dogs with pendulous ears benefit from a weekly "airing out." Pull the ears back over the dog's head or behind the neck and tape them in place for a few hours. This looks funny, but it can prevent ear problems down the road.

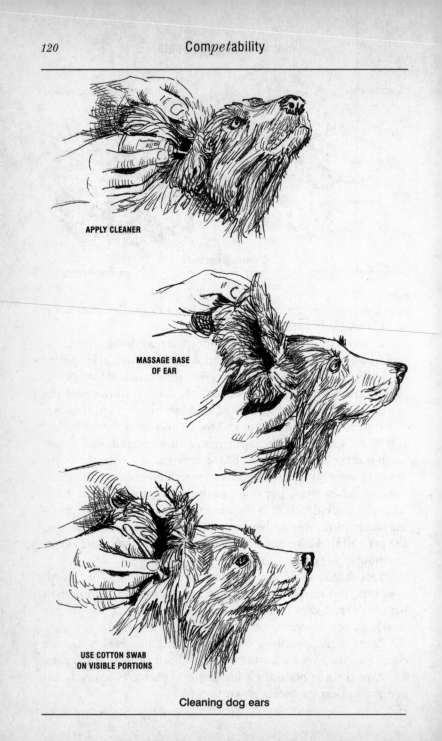

APPLY CLEANER

MASSAGE BASE
OF EAR

USE COTTON SWAB
ON VISIBLE PORTIONS

Cleaning dog ears

Dog breeds like Poodles, Cocker Spaniels, Schnauzers, Lhasa Apsos, Bouvier des Flandres, and Old English Sheepdogs actually have hair growing inside their ears that can block circulation and holds moisture. Every one to three months you should clip the hair around the ears (use electric clippers, not scissors) and pluck the fur growing inside the ears to allow air to enter. Many owners are able to carry out this service for their dogs, but this is a procedure best demonstrated first by your veterinarian or professional groomer.

Dental Care

Dogs and cats often suffer from dental problems. Just like their owners, pets can develop plaque and tartar, which can lead to periodontal disease and decay. Bad breath is the most obvious sign of this (other symptoms are listed in Chapter 11).

The teeth of wolves and wildcats remain relatively clean because their diet is unprocessed and raw. Chewing through fur, skin, bone, and flesh naturally scrubs the tooth surfaces clean. But the canned and kibbled foods that domestic dogs and cats eat, though they provide complete and balanced nutrition, do little for dental hygiene.

Canned food tends to stick to the teeth. A dry diet may help keep teeth cleaner, but dogs and cats don't chew their food all that much. They tend to swallow it in chunks without the "detergent" benefit people get from munching on crisp foods like apples. Feeding your pet table scraps or sugary treats will make the problem even worse. Dental problems vary between individuals as well; small dog breeds like the Chihuahua, Maltese, Shih Tzu, and Yorkshire Terrier are the most prone to dental problems.

Professional cleaning by your veterinarian is recommended for all cats and dogs once or twice a year. The frequency of professional dentistry can be reduced by brushing your pets' teeth at home. A once-a-week cleaning is a good plan.

Don't use human products; the flavor of our toothpaste, as well as the foaming action, is distasteful to pets. Dogs and cats cannot spit, so they must swallow the paste, and the high fluoride levels in human products may contribute to kidney damage in pets when the foam is swallowed. Pet toothpastes that don't foam are available at pet stores, and they have appealing flavors like beef, poultry, and malt.

A human toothbrush designed for infants may be appropriate for medium to large dogs. Special pet toothbrushes in smaller sizes with softer bristles are appropriate for cats and tiny dogs. Finger toothbrushes with tiny rubber bristles are available; they slip over the owner's finger and are accepted more readily by pets than sticking a toothbrush in their mouth.

To accustom your dog and cat to dental care, start by simply stroking the pet's cheek and chin. Cats in particular like this. Stroke the dog's lips and handle the cat's mouth for short periods of time, and stop if the pet protests too much. Progress to slipping a finger inside the mouth and rubbing the teeth. Typically, the inside surface of the teeth will stay cleaner because of the tongue action, so you can concentrate on the outside surface; that way you don't need to force the mouth open, which most pets protest. Try flavoring your finger with beef broth for dogs or tuna water for cats. Just be careful the pet doesn't mistake your finger for a treat and chomp down on it.

Then proceed to a soft cloth wrapped around your finger, or to the finger toothbrush. Spread the pet toothpaste on the implement and massage the teeth and gums for as long as your pet will tolerate it. You don't have to finish at one sitting; you can continue another time. Dental rinses with antibacterial properties that help prevent plaque buildup, promote healing, and control bad breath are also available.

Dogs, which are more mouth-oriented anyway, are much more accepting of tooth attention than cats. The trick is to convince the pet, especially a reluctant cat, that the attention is pleasant and rewarding. Always end sessions with praise and perhaps a play period.

Eye Care

Flat-faced cats like Persians and some dog breeds like Poodles and Maltese have large, prominent eyes that tend to water. The tears should flow into the tear ducts and be carried away, but sometimes tearing is too excessive or the ducts are too narrow.

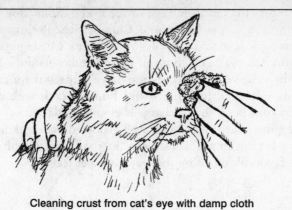

Cleaning crust from cat's eye with damp cloth

This becomes problematic because tears can stain the pet's face at the inside corner beneath the eyes, particularly in white or light-colored dogs and cats. The dried tears can encrust the fur, irritate the skin, and lead to infection. By cleaning your pet's eyes each day, you can prevent these problems. Simply soak a cotton ball or soft cloth in warm water or contact lens saline solution, place it for a moment against the crusty fur to soften the secretion, and then wipe the deposit away. To treat stained fur beneath the eyes, you can use one part hydrogen peroxide diluted in five parts water on a cotton ball, but *be very careful not to get the solution in your pet's eyes.* Commercial preparations available at pet stores will also help remove the stain from fur.

In dog breeds that have lots of nasal folds near the eye, like the Pekingese, Pug, and Bulldog, the hairs that grow near the eye may cause irritation and excessive watering when they come in contact with the eye itself. Keep long hair in these areas clipped with electric clippers to prevent eye irritation. If you don't feel comfortable doing this, ask your groomer or vet. In wrinkle-skinned pets like Bulldogs and "Peke-faced" Persians, you'll want to wipe out the skin folds regularly with the 1:5 hydrogen peroxide and water solution on a cotton ball or swab to help prevent skin irritation or infection.

Cocker Spaniels, Weimaraners, and Golden Retrievers seem to be prone to eyelashes growing in the wrong location—on the inside rather than outside edge of the eyelid. Some dog breeds, including the Chow Chow and Chinese Shar-Pei, may suffer from entropion, in which eyelids roll inward, causing eye irritation from the eyelashes. Both of these conditions must be corrected by your veterinarian. Normal eye secretions for cats and dogs are clear and liquid, just like human tears; seek medical help for your pet if the discharge is cloudy or dark.

Keeping your cat and dog well groomed and looking good will prevent health problems down the road, and will ultimately have a favorable effect on the way your pet feels.

CHAPTER NINE

Dogs Mope, Cats Hide

Our cats and dogs are subject to many of the same illnesses and conditions their human owners suffer. But pets are at a severe disadvantage compared to people. We know when we feel ill, and we can call on a doctor for help. Furthermore, we can tell the doctor what hurts and how long we've felt bad, and we can even offer an idea about the reason for our illness.

Dogs and cats have only limited means to tell us when they feel bad, and they certainly aren't able to explain how we can help them. There's a subtle distinction in veterinary terminology to account for this. People are said to have *symptoms* of illness, because we can actually talk about how we're feeling. Pets, who can't tell us how they feel, are instead said to have *signs* of ill health. These signs are the best clues owners have to recognize illness in their pets. Dogs and cats may react differently: when they feel bad, dogs typically mope, whereas cats hide. Felines find a secluded spot—say, beneath the bed—and stay out of sight. Dogs assume a dejected posture in the middle of a room in plain view of owners and sometimes sigh and moan mournfully.

SOCIAL SUPPORT SYSTEM

As inherently social beings, dogs are concerned with the welfare of their pack, and that concern extends to all of the individuals that make up the pack. Healthy wolves not only protect and care for the young but also provide food for their injured or ill brethren, and it's no different with dogs. That may be why there are so many tales of altruistic behavior by dogs. To the dog, the social group to which he belongs—his family—is the most important thing in the world. But this caring attitude can extend beyond his immediate family group as well.

Dogs seem to know it's important to alert members of their family group to their distress. Between canine pack members, there are minute sounds and chemical signals—certain scents the ill dog's body gives off—that alert other animals but are not noticeable to human owners. And since most modern canine social groups include human owners, the injured or sick dog points out his problems to people in more obvious ways.

Typically, dogs that feel ill seek comfort and companionship from family members. They may whine, whimper, hold up a hurt paw, or simply stare soulfully into your eyes.

LIVING ALONE

Cats, on the other hand, all too often hide their distress so well that owners don't notice anything is wrong with the cat until it's too late to help. The cat tends to keep her own counsel when she doesn't feel well. Unlike the dog, which has a social support system, the adult cat relies on herself. She will protect and defend her offspring as vigorously as the canine and will coexist in an extended social group made up of other felines, but for the cat, illness is a sign of weakness that puts her at a decided disadvantage. She can no longer defend her territory, and so she risks becoming prey for some other predator willing to take advantage of her debilitated state. For the wild feline, losing claim to feline "property" and status, with its attendant hunting rights, can literally mean death. Therefore, the injured or ill cat does everything possible to remain invisible and not draw attention to herself. The wild feline will often find a safe hiding place and try to wait it out until she self-heals. The house cat does the same, disappearing into the darkest, most inaccessible spot.

Of course, there are always exceptions; some dogs withdraw from social contact when ill, while cats may loudly proclaim their discomfort. But overall, dogs evolved to seek solace in their family groups, and so they seek attention from owners when they feel sick. Cats evolved to depend on themselves, and so they typically keep to themselves when they're ill.

If you live with both cats and dogs, it's not unusual for the squeaky wheel, the pet that demands the most attention, to receive just that. The more retiring or stoic a pet is, the less likely you will notice anything is amiss, at least not right away. Pet owners who have both cats and dogs must maintain a high level of vigilance in order to notice pet problems and seek a timely solution.

TELLTALE ELIMINATION

Your pet's waste products offer the most obvious signs of good or poor health. It is important for you to be aware of what normal pet waste looks like, even if your pets take care of their business outdoors.

Be aware, though, that some cats and dogs tend to be quite shy when it comes to doing their duty—they don't want an audience. Hovering over them may prompt some pets to avoid eliminating until the situation reaches the critical stage, and this may even predispose some pets to constipation. Provide your pets with privacy, and check out the deposit only after they've finished. Put your dog in his fenced yard, and watch from a window—or, use a long leash to give him distance, and turn your head away until he's done. There are "privacy screens" to place around the shy feline's litter box.

Often a break in house training—an accident in the house—is a sign that something is wrong. For instance, your pet may urinate on the carpet if he suffers from an infection like cystitis or develops diabetes, which can increase urine production. Any number of viral infections can result in gastrointestinal upset, so that the dog or cat must defecate immediately rather than waiting to reach the yard or the litter box. Stress can also result in hit-or-miss bathroom behavior.

How often should you check your pet's stool? If you have an indoor cat, you'll examine Kitty's health every time you clean the litter box. If your dogs have access to a confined outdoor space, you will need to clean up the yard frequently. A cursory look every couple of days is a good idea. And for dogs or cats that use the whole of the great outdoors as their toilet, you'll need to make a point to check them out. It's easier on you, fairer to your neighbors, and safer for your pets to limit outdoor excursions to a confined space and to prevent roaming.

Normal stool is firm and medium brown, but the color can vary depending on the diet. Some canned foods, because they have a greater percentage of liquid, may result in softer stools than will a dry diet. A soft stool, runny diarrhea, excessive mucus, or even blood can be a sign of a wide variety of conditions, from a simple tummy upset or intestinal parasite to a deadly virus.

Constipation, which can indicate anything from a hairball to a lethal intestinal blockage, is another condition that can be discovered by monitoring the yard and the litter box. The number of bowel movements each day will again be determined by your pet's diet. A decrease in the amount or frequency of bowel movements should alert you that all is not well.

Most cases of diarrhea and constipation are transitory. Pets may simply eat something that doesn't agree with them. For instance, dogs often rummage in the garbage and as a consequence may have an upset tummy. Cats often swallow bugs or other small game that upsets their digestion, and both dogs and cats may swallow inedible objects, like buttons or stones. Dogs, especially, tend to scavenge even as adults.

Normal urine is yellow to amber in color. Excessive urination can be a sign of metabolic disease or even poisoning. Blood in the urine is an obvious sign of problems.

EATING AND DRINKING HABITS

Just like people, cats or dogs that don't feel well may lose their appetite. Loss of appetite, or even an outright refusal to eat, can again be caused by a variety of conditions from innocuous to potentially fatal. It's particularly important to realize that dogs can go for two or three days without a meal (remember that they are gorgers) without too much distress. If the dog feels and acts well otherwise, give him a day or three to get his appetite back, but it if goes on longer, consult a veterinarian.

The opposite is true for cats. Feline fasting, or simply eating substantially less for a long period of time, can have devastating complications that can kill the cat. Kittens shouldn't go without food for more than eighteen to twenty-four hours, and adult cats—especially overweight felines—should go no longer than thirty-six to forty-eight hours without food. See a veterinarian immediately if your cat refuses to eat for an extended period of time.

Overeating can also be an indication of illness. Remember that many dogs, particularly some of the hunting breeds, will overeat given the chance. Some cats will, too, and under normal circumstances the result will be only an unhealthy gain of weight. But when your cat or dog is ravenous all the time, yet doesn't gain weight or even loses it, a metabolic disorder like diabetes may be the cause. Only growing or pregnant animals should gain weight. Otherwise, any clear fluctuation in weight should be diagnosed by a veterinarian to determine if there are health problems. In cats, a noticeable swelling of the abdomen can be a sign of a deadly infectious disorder called feline infectious peritonitis (described further in Chapter 10).

Drinking excessive amounts of water is another sign of possible illness. While pets require more water on hot days, a water bowl that goes dry too often may indicate anything from antifreeze poisoning to diabetes to kidney disease.

As with people, vomiting can be another sign of illness. It can be caused by a wide range of problems, the worst being deadly viral diseases. However, vomiting and regurgitation are not at all uncommon and don't always mean the pet is sick.

How can you tell the difference? Regurgitation happens within only a few minutes of eating and is an involuntary reflex that expels undigested food. Cats often regurgitate food that is too cold, and dogs may regurgitate food if they gulp it down too quickly. Simply warming the food to room temperature will stop the problem with cats. Your dogs' eating pace can be slowed down by feeding them alone or by dropping a large, nonswallowable ball in the bowl so that they have to eat around it.

Vomiting occurs when food has been in the stomach for some time and is at least partially digested. If the stomach is empty, vomiting will bring up digestive fluids without food. It is normal for cats occasionally to spit up a hairball; proper grooming will help alleviate this problem. Some dogs seem prone to vomiting frothy yellow material, particularly early in the morning before they've eaten. Feeding a small meal when Poochie first gets up may help settle his stomach.

Vomiting can also be a symptom of several life-threatening illnesses in both cats and dogs, however. If vomiting continues for longer than twenty-four hours, especially if it's accompanied by diarrhea or lethargy, take your pet to a veterinarian.

BODY WORKS

Because cats and dogs are such sensory creatures, anything that interferes with their eyes, ears, or nose can make them feel miserable. Runny eyes and discharge from the ears are both signs of illness, as is walking in circles or tilting and holding the head to one side. Coughing, wheezing, and sneezing are also signs of trouble that could range from allergies to congestive heart failure.

Both dogs and cats go through life nose-first, sniffing and snorting all sorts of interesting smells. But along with scent, they may also inhale foreign material. One of the most common routes of viral and bacterial infection is through the nose. Normally, cats' and dogs' noses are moist, with possibly a small amount of clear fluid. If the amount is excessive, and particularly if it's cloudy or thick, then it is an abnormal discharge.

A stuffy nose by itself can pose a risk for cats. The smell of food prompts the cat to eat, and nasal discharge will kill the cat's appetite. Refusing to eat can make a marginally ill cat even sicker. A humidifier or steam from a shower will help open nasal passages; use a warm, damp cloth to soften and wipe away the discharge. Adding a bit of warm water to food, warming it in the microwave to body temperature (102°F), or spiking it with a drizzle of chicken broth or meat baby food may prompt the anorectic pet to eat.

SCRATCHING THE SURFACE

The skin is the largest organ of all and, as the protective outer covering, is the first line of the body's defense. Normal skin is smooth and light tan or pink; dark-colored pets may have some areas of pigmented skin.

Itchy skin is not normal and typically is a sign of an allergic reaction or irritation which can be caused by fleas, hot spots, or other things. Continuous scratching, which produces the thumping noise that keeps you awake at night, is the dog or cat's attempt to relieve irritation. Itchiness is often accompanied by reddened, inflamed, and scabby skin. Scratching isn't limited to flailing rear legs, either. Dogs seem to mimic cats when they rub their heads and faces against furniture or continuously lick themselves to relieve an itch. The saliva from excessive licking can discolor the skin from a normal clear pink to steel gray.

Any lump or bump is a cause for concern. Cats and dogs get a variety of cancers, and the lump or bump found on a cat has a much higher chance of being cancer than one found on a dog. As with human cancers, early detection is the key to successful treatment, so if you find a suspect skin problem, report it immediately to your veterinarian.

Thinning fur or hair loss, not to be confused with shedding, is another sure sign that something is wrong.

One of the best barometers of feline health is the cat's grooming behavior. Cats that don't feel well often stop grooming themselves, resulting in what's called an unthrifty appearance. In other words, the spit-and-polish look is gone; the fur is dry or greasy, dingy, and unkempt. Letting their appearance go can indicate almost any kind of health upset, from physical to emotional, and may commonly be accompanied by other signs as well—anything from loss of appetite to diarrhea.

OBVIOUS OMENS AND SUBTLE SIGNS

Every pet owner should learn to recognize certain signs of distress that are a red flag saying "Emergency!" These signs include bleeding, difficulty breathing, and loss of consciousness, and may result from any number of causes, from being hit by a car or falling from a high perch to drowning or poisoning.

Each pet reacts differently to pain. Typically, the quiet pet becomes more vocal while the outgoing pet becomes reticent. Pain can prompt the cat to hide and refuse to move, while the dog yelps and holds up his leg. Drooling or panting can also indicate discomfort, and the cat or dog in pain may shiver and tremble, then flinch or strike out with tooth or claw when touched. Stomachache is typically shown by the cat or dog hunching its back and walking stiffly.

When cats and dogs share the same home, they are often able to reveal things about each other's health status that owners would otherwise not notice. The dog can be a barometer of feline health, and vice versa. If Kitty hisses and swats at Poochie during a game of tag that they both usually enjoy, it might be a one-time quirk, or it could indicate something's wrong. Maybe the cat has an abscess brewing and is indicating that being tagged is painful.

Perhaps Old Fogy Dog stops objecting to Junior Kitty playing with his tail the way he usually does. Has he gotten used to the precocious feline? Maybe. But perhaps it's painful for him to move out of the way, so he's become resigned to putting up with the cat's antics.

Cats and dogs who have grown close to each other are often sensitive to each other's feelings. Cats may purr and snuggle close to the arthritic dog, while dogs may search worriedly about for a sick feline friend who has hidden herself away.

Despite the popularity and availability of do-it-yourself guides, treating your cat's or dog's symptoms yourself without first checking with a veterinarian is foolish at best and dangerous at worst. Even if you have cat- or dog-specific medicine, you may be mistaken about the cause of the symptoms, and you could do more harm than good. Be particularly careful about using medicine intended for humans on your dog or cat. Although some may be appropriate, the dosage is often very different than what you'd think; other times, what's safe for you may not be for your pet. For instance, a human antidiarrheal medication may be toxic to the pet; even if it works and relieves the immediate signs, diarrhea will return unless the actual cause is determined. And if the cause is a deadly virus, the pet may die while you're trying to treat the symptom.

Recognizing signs of illness in your cats and dogs is extremely important, but it's equally critical to understand what each symptom means. Only then can the appropriate treatment begin.

CHAPTER TEN

Kennel Cough and Cat Colds

Although a veterinarian is essential when your pet is sick, even healthy cats and dogs should see a veterinarian every year. Very young pets and elderly pets require more frequent veterinary attention. Annual examinations can find and treat health problems before they become troublesome or dangerous. Many of the deadly viral diseases of cats and dogs are preventable with appropriate vaccinations, and special medications can prevent parasites from making your pets sick.

It's not possible within the scope of this chapter to catalog every single disease and condition that afflicts cats and dogs, but some of their most common and important health problems are discussed here. Becoming familiar with these conditions, their signs, and the appropriate treatments will help you keep your peaceable kingdom healthy and happy.

CANINE BLOAT

Bloat is just what it sounds like: a painful swelling of the stomach with gas and/or fluid. Unless emergency relief is available, the dog can die.

All dogs are susceptible to bloat, but it usually afflicts large deep-chested breeds like the Saint Bernard, German Shepherd, and Labrador Retriever, and the sufferers are usually males between four and seven years old. The cause is not clearly understood, but gulping large amounts of air while eating or drinking may contribute to the condition. Dogs afflicted with bloat typically eat a lot, drink lots of water after eating, then exercise vigorously two to three hours after meals.

Bloat is deadly because the stomach becomes twisted, and the gas and food are trapped inside it like air in an overinflated balloon, so the painful swelling can't be relieved by either vomiting or burping. The twisting can ultimately shut off the blood supply to the stomach and spleen.

Signs are extreme restlessness, excessive drooling, and unsuccessful attempts to vomit or defecate. The stomach swells and is painful to the touch; the dog breathes rapidly, has pale, cold gums, and may collapse. If your dog displays any one or several of these symptoms, get him to the veterinarian immediately.

X-rays may be needed to confirm the diagnosis. Treatment includes passing a stomach tube down the dog's throat and into the stomach to allow the gas to escape. When the stomach is too severely twisted to allow this passage, surgery is required. About 30 to 60 percent of dogs with severe bloat will die. Dogs that recover need proper dietary management and sometimes surgery to prevent recurrence.

To reduce the risk of bloat, discourage your dog from gorging, especially if he's a higher-risk breed. Feed him three or four small meals throughout the day rather than one or two big meals. Moistening the dog's kibble may reduce his urge to drink huge quantities of water following a meal. In particular, enforce a rest period for at least one hour after each meal.

CANINE PARVOVIRUS (CPV)

One of the deadliest and most contagious viral diseases of dogs is canine parvovirus disease, which has been around since about 1976. It's believed the virus mutated from a related virus of wildlife or perhaps even from the feline parvovirus (panleukopenia). Sick dogs shed the virus in their droppings, and the disease is spread by contact with infected feces.

The virus can live for at least five months, probably longer, in the environment. This means that your dog can be exposed after you've walked through a contaminated area and carried the virus home on your shoes. Dogs contract the virus by sniffing and licking their immediate environs. They become sick within two weeks of exposure.

All dogs are at risk, but puppies are the most severely affected and have the highest mortality rate. The parvovirus is drawn to the body's rapidly dividing cells, and it attacks them specifically. In particular, the nutrition-absorbing cells that line the intestines are in the line of fire and, in rarer instances, the heart muscle itself.

The more common intestinal form can develop within hours. Some dogs may exhibit stomach pain by hunching and may become lethargic, then die quite suddenly. But the signs usually include high fever, up to 106°F, vomiting, and bloody diarrhea that has a rotten odor. Because the lining of the intestines is being killed and sloughed out in the diarrhea, the body cannot process water and food. The subsequent dehydration and shock cause the dog's death. Veterinary hospitalization is necessary if the dog is to survive.

Treatment focuses on fluid therapy along with medications to control the vomiting and diarrhea. Food and water are withheld during this initial period to rest the damaged digestive tract. Once the diarrhea and vomiting have stopped, bland foods and water are offered in small servings several times a day. If the dog can survive the initial infection, the intestinal tract will heal and again be able to process nutrients.

During convalescence, the sick dog must be isolated from other dogs to prevent spread of the disease. Everything—bedding, food bowls, toys—must be disinfected. Canine parvovirus is resistant to most household disinfectants but can be killed using chlorine bleach. Dilute 1 part Clorox in 30 parts water to create a suitable disinfectant. Don't forget to disinfect yourself— hands, shoes, and whatever else has come in contact with the infected dog. Appropriate vaccination will prevent the disease (discussed at the end of this chapter).

FELINE PANLEUKOPENIA VIRUS (FPV)

This disease, which used to be referred to as feline distemper, is actually a type of parvovirus. Though all cats are at risk, most often the disease affects kittens. The virus is spread by cat-to-cat contact through infected saliva, vomit, urine, and feces. Cats can also contract the disease from contaminated food bowls, litter boxes, and bedding and even their owners' hands.

Symptoms appear two to ten days after exposure and last about a week. The virus attacks the most rapidly reproducing cells of the body, which in adult cats are in the intestinal lining. But in young kittens, the brain is often affected, causing infected kittens to lose coordination and shake or twitch uncontrollably.

Typical signs of FPV are sudden high fever and loss of appetite, with vomiting and diarrhea. An afflicted cat will have stomach pain and may crouch with her head between her paws and cry. Mortality is high, even in adult cats; kittens may die within twelve hours following the first symptoms.

Signs of illness are usually enough to allow a veterinarian to diagnose the disease, but sometimes laboratory tests are used to confirm diagnosis. Like canine parvovirus, once a cat is infected with FPV, there's no specific treatment; the cat's own body must rally and heal itself. Some measures can be taken to buy the cat time to heal, however; the veterinarian can provide fluid therapy and sometimes blood transfusions, along with medicine to control vomiting and diarrhea. If the cat survives the first week, she'll usually recover, but a convalescing cat will continue to shed the virus for up to six weeks and so will have to be isolated from healthy cats to prevent the spread of the infection. Highly effective preventive vaccinations are available (discussed at the end of this chapter).

CANINE HEPATITIS

Yes, dogs can get hepatitis, but it is not the same disease that affects people, and it's not transmissible to people. Canine infectious hepatitis is an extremely contagious disease caused by a virus. The word "hepatitis" means "liver inflammation," but the canine virus also infects the dog's kidneys and the lining of the blood vessels. Puppies are most severely affected, but any dog is susceptible.

The disease is spread when healthy dogs come in contact with infected waste, eat or drink after an infected dog, or even breathe the same air. Within only a few days of exposure, the virus spreads throughout the dog's body and multiplies in the tissues, saliva, urine, and feces.

A wide range of signs can appear, but the *fatal fulminating form* of the disease may have no signs at all before the dog dies. In other cases a dog may suddenly become sick with bloody diarrhea, then collapse and die. Some dogs simply act lethargic.

In the *acute form* of hepatitis, the dog typically refuses to eat and may vomit blood; a high fever will develop (up to 106°F), accompanied by extreme thirst and bloody diarrhea. Because of a painfully swollen liver, the dog will assume a hunched posture and move as little as possible. Jaundice—a yellowing of the tissues—sometimes develops; it is seen in the yellow-tinged whites of the eyes or the inside of the ears.

Canine infectious hepatitis is usually diagnosed simply on the basis of the characteristic signs, but the disease can be confirmed by blood tests. Treatment depends on the severity of the illness and will many times require veterinary hospitalization. Antibiotics are given to prevent further complication, and vitamin supplementation may be required until the liver recovers enough to start producing them again. The dog's throat can become so inflamed that it hurts for him to eat, and fluid therapy helps provide necessary nutrition and fights dehydration that can result from diarrhea and vomiting. Even dogs that recover from the disease may remain infectious and shed the virus in their urine for several months. The best way to prevent canine infectious hepatitis is to vaccinate the dog each year (discussed at the end of this chapter).

FATTY LIVER DISEASE

The most common liver disease in cats is feline hepatic lipidosis. The condition is often referred to as fatty liver disease because it's caused by the deposit of fat cells that interfere with the liver's function. The exact mechanism of the disease isn't known, and any cat can develop the syndrome; however, almost all of its victims are fat middle-aged cats. The disease is triggered when the cat stops eating. When the liver stops working, Kitty feels even worse, so she continues to refuse food, prompting even more fat to travel into the liver. The vicious cycle results in the cat literally starving to death as the liver fails.

Fatty liver disease is generally diagnosed simply from the signs: not eating, lethargy, and sometimes jaundice. The principal treatment is forcing the cat to eat, or force-feeding, which is usually necessary if the cat is to survive. A feeding tube is surgically placed directly into the stomach, either routed through the abdominal wall, down the nose and into the stomach, or through the cat's throat to the stomach. The cat is fed a highly nutritious soft diet through the tube three or four times a day. Cats may also require other medications to help the liver recover from the ordeal.

Feeding makes the cat feel better almost immediately, and recovery can take place at home with the owner continuing to tube-feed as instructed by the veterinarian. It may be several weeks before the cat is willing to eat again on her own. Because almost all sufferers are fat, the best way to avoid fatty liver disease is to prevent feline obesity.

CORONAVIRUS

Canine coronavirus is an intestinal disease similar to parvovirus but usually less severe. The disease is very contagious, however, and is spread by contact with infected feces or saliva. Any dog can contract the virus, but puppies are most severely affected.

Signs are also similar to those of parvovirus. They include depression, loss of appetite, vomiting, and diarrhea that may or may not contain blood. The stool is loose, foul-smelling, and often yellow-orange. However, some infected dogs show no signs at all.

Treatment is the same as for parvovirus, but the disease is often so mild that the dog will recover in about ten days even without specific treatment. By itself, canine coronavirus is rarely fatal. But it's not uncommon for the virus to infect dogs at the same time as parvovirus, and the combination can be deadly. A vaccination is available, though not always given. Discuss this vaccination with your veterinarian.

FELINE INFECTIOUS PERITONITIS (FIP)

Caused by a feline coronavirus, FIP attacks the blood vessels throughout the cat's body, especially those of the organs in the abdomen. Cats contract this virus by breathing or swallowing it during close contact with an infected cat. Cats who live in multi-cat homes or catteries or who roam outdoors are at highest risk because they're exposed most often. You can kill the virus by spraying or washing the environment with a solution of 4 ounces of bleach diluted in 1 gallon of water.

The early signs of this disease are quite vague; they include fever, depression, loss of appetite, and/or weight loss. Later signs are more distinct and characterize two forms of the disease. The signs of the "wet" form of the disease include a painless swelling of the abdomen, which occurs when the escaping fluid from the damaged vessels accumulates in the abdomen. Sometimes the cat will show signs of jaundice—a yellowing of the inside of the ears or the whites of the eyes—if the liver is affected.

The signs of the "dry" form are less obvious; they include weight loss and anemia. Cats infected with this form will sometimes lose control of their hind legs or suffer personality changes or eye disease. Cats with the dry form may survive a year or longer after signs first develop, but those with the wet form typically live only three or four months after signs emerge.

The disease is diagnosed primarily through visible symptoms. Laboratory tests can detect coronavirus, but they cannot tell the difference between the FIP variety and those that are relatively harmless. Only microscopic evaluation of a tissue sample can determine for sure if the cat has FIP.

Anti-inflammatory medication along with antibiotics may help slow the progression of the virus, and good nutrition will help the cat feel better, but there is no cure for FIP. In most cases, owners elect to end the cat's suffering through euthanasia before the terminal stages of the disease are reached. Vaccines are available to help prevent FIP infection, but many experts question their effectiveness. Preventing exposure is the best way to protect cats from FIP.

DISTEMPER

Distemper is the number one killer of pet dogs throughout the world. It is caused by a virus similar to the human measles virus, but while it's highly contagious among dogs, it does not affect people.

The virus is transmitted through the air and by contaminated objects the same way a human cold virus spreads. Most dogs will be exposed to distemper at some point during their lifetime, and it can kill a dog at any age, though puppies are more susceptible than adult dogs.

The virus attacks the cells that line the surfaces of the body organs; it affects the skin, eyes, intestines, nose, lungs, and even the brain. Symptoms begin developing six to nine days following exposure. The severity of the disease varies from mild to extremely severe and depends a great deal on how healthy the dog is to begin with.

Early signs include a fever of 103°F to 105°F, loss of appetite, lethargy, and runny eyes and nose. The watery eye and nose discharge soon thickens to a sticky yellow drainage, and yellowish diarrhea may develop. Over the next week or so, the dog may seem to improve, only to relapse soon after. Some cases of distemper attack the skin, resulting in pus-filled blisters and lesions similar to those seen in people with measles; the nose and footpads may turn thick and callused. If the virus reaches the brain, the dog may suffer seizures or uncontrollable jerking, twitching, or chewing movements. Even dogs that survive distemper may be left with uncontrollable muscle or limb jerking or periodic seizures that result from damage to the central nervous system.

A diagnosis can usually be based on the symptoms. There is no cure available for distemper, and in most cases supportive treatment in a veterinary hospital is necessary if a dog is to survive. Fluid therapy, antidiarrheal medication, and antiseizure medication may be given. The disease is highly preventable with the appropriate annual vaccinations.

HIP DYSPLASIA

Hip dysplasia is an abnormality of the hipbones. Almost exclusive to larger breed dogs like German Shepherds, Saint Bernards, and Greater Swiss Mountain Dogs, it is the most common cause of rear-end lameness in dogs.

In a normal hip the ball of the thighbone (femur) fits into the socket of the pelvis. In dysplasia, a combination of slack muscles and a shallow hip socket allows the connection to work loose. This results in abnormal wear on the joint, causing further wear and tear on the bone.

The condition is painful, and dogs suffering from dysplasia typically limp, have an odd wavery gait or "bunny hop," and find it difficult to rise, run, and jump. Severe cases are usually apparent by the age of nine months; some dogs, however, never show signs at all. Hip dysplasia can be inherited, but even dogs with normal parents can develop hip dysplasia.

Diagnosis is made using X-rays of the pelvis and hips. There is no cure for this bone disorder. Treatment attempts to relieve pain and improve the function of the joint, but success depends on the severity of the problem.

Extreme cases may require surgery to alter the muscles and tendons to reduce pain, rebuild bone, or sometimes remove the "ball" to allow the dog's body to create a new "false" joint from tissue. Sometimes total hip replacement is performed; the entire ball-and-socket joint is replaced by a stainless-steel prosthesis similar to the one used in humans.

Mild to moderate cases of dysplasia can often be managed by giving the dog pain relievers such as buffered aspirin, but only as prescribed by the vet. Dogs with dysplasia should be encouraged to continue moderate exercise to improve muscle tone, which will help to reduce the painful wear and tear on the joint. Excessive weight will also put increased strain on the joints, so dogs with this condition should remain lean. Most dogs with hip dysplasia can lead happy, otherwise healthy lives, as long as their owner remains vigilant regarding their special needs.

KENNEL COUGH

Kennel cough is a highly contagious inflammation of the dog's tracheobronchial system, which affects the larynx or upper throat, the trachea, and the bronchi (tubes leading to the lungs).

Kennel cough can be caused by several different infectious agents working alone or in combination. The most common agents are bacteria called *Bordetella bronchiseptica,* the canine parainfluenza virus, and the canine adenovirus-2. These agents attach themselves to the delicate hairlike cilia of the dog's trachea, which irritates the dog's respiratory tract. A stressful condition like overcrowding, drafts, or poor nutrition may make the dog more susceptible. Although most cases are mild, kennel cough in puppies can cause stunted lung development, and up to 20 percent of cases caused by canine adenovirus-2 develop into pneumonia.

Occasionally, there may be a discharge from the eyes and nose, and some dogs experience fever and loss of appetite. But most often, kennel cough is characterized by a "honking" cough that can be prompted by gentle pressure on the outside of the dog's throat. The signs can last from a few days to several weeks.

Infectious agents reside in the saliva and nasal secretions, and are transmitted through the air by coughing or by direct nose-to-nose contact. The disease is so named because the close proximity of dogs in kennels or at shows promotes the disease.

Diagnosis is based on the dog's recent history and clinical signs. Treatment depends on what caused the condition. Because the disease results in a vicious cycle of irritation causing the cough, and cough causing further irritation, medications to relieve persistent coughing are very important. Anti-inflammatory drugs and drugs to help the dog breathe may also be prescribed. When there is a chance of secondary infection, antibiotics can be helpful. Preventive vaccinations are available.

FELINE UPPER RESPIRATORY INFECTION (URI)

The signs of feline upper respiratory infection, commonly referred to as cat colds, are very similar to human flu or cold symptoms. The human and feline illnesses are caused by very different agents, however, and cannot be transmitted between species.

Like canine kennel cough, upper respiratory infection can be caused by several different infectious agents, alone or in combination with one another. In most cases it's not necessary to determine which agent is causing the problem, because the treatment for each is so similar. The two agents that cause 80 percent of the infections are feline viral rhinotracheitis (a kind of herpesvirus) and calicivirus. A primitive bacteria called *Chlamydia cati* also accounts for some infections.

Cats catch URIs by coming into direct contact with an infected cat's saliva or nasal or eye discharge. Sneezing also spreads infection, as does contact with a contaminated litter box, cage, or food bowl. The infection can even be carried on an owner's hands after petting the cat. Cats living in catteries, shelters, or some multi-cat homes simply pass the disease back and forth to one another.

The most common symptoms are sneezing, stuffy nose, and watering eyes. Painful ulcers in the mouth and nose may develop, and when chlamydia is present, small blisters may erupt on the surface of the cat's eyes. The greatest danger is to kittens, but the infection can turn into pneumonia and become deadly even in adults. Because cats rely on the smell of food to stimulate their appetite, upper respiratory infections that plug the nose and interfere with the sense of smell may keep cats from eating, which can make them even sicker.

No effective medication is available to cure URI. Treatment may include fluid therapy, medicated ointments and drops to soothe ulcerated tissues, and a humidifier to soften nasal and eye secretions. Probably the single most important care is the nursing an owner does at home, particularly prompting the cat to continue to eat. Preventive vaccinations are available and are quite effective.

CANINE LEPTOSPIROSIS

Leptospirosis is transmitted by highly contagious bacteria found in the urine of infected animals. Dogs catch the disease after contact with infected urine from cows, sheep, or wild animals—rats seem to be the most common source of infection. The bacteria can also be transmitted from infected dogs to people.

These bacteria infect the dog by entering through a break in the skin or when the dog swallows contaminated water or food. Most cases of canine leptospirosis are mild, but symptoms—high fever with listlessness, severe diarrhea, vomiting, loss of appetite, increased thirst, and increased urination—can become severe, and the disease may result in kidney damage. Pain in the kidneys may cause the dog to walk in a hunched posture. Mouth ulcers can make eating painful, and a brownish coating may appear on the tongue. Occasionally, when the liver is affected, a yellow tinge (jaundice) will be seen in the eyes, gums, and tongue.

Diagnosis can be confirmed by finding the bacteria in the dog's urine or blood sample. When leptospirosis is diagnosed early and treated aggressively, most dogs can be expected to make a complete recovery. The bacteria are killed using a combination of antibiotic therapies. Fluid therapy to reduce dehydration, along with medication to control vomiting and diarrhea, may be required. In many cases the dog must be hospitalized and treated under quarantine; this not only allows the illness to be adequately treated but also helps prevent transmission of the disease to people. The bacteria can remain in the urine for as long as a year following infection.

To reduce the chance for human infection when your dog is recovering at home, wash your hands thoroughly with soapy warm water after handling the dog. Confine the dog away from where you eat your meals.

The disease can be prevented by having the dog vaccinated.

FELINE LEUKEMIA VIRUS (FELV)

FeLV is the number one killer of pet cats. It leads to a number of diseases. Leukemia, or cancer of the blood, is only one cancer caused by FeLV; others include lymphosarcoma and a number of bone marrow cancers. The virus also weakens and may eventually destroy the immune system, which makes the infected cat so vulnerable that any illness—even an otherwise innocuous problem—can become fatal.

Because the virus may give rise to a huge range of illnesses, the symptoms are incredibly varied. Danger signals include loss of weight, poor appetite, bloody diarrhea, recurring colds, and mouth or claw-bed sores. Cats contract FeLV from contact with infected saliva, feces, or urine, from sharing food bowls and litter pans, or from grooming one another. All cats are at risk, but those having contact with other cats become sick most often.

FeLV is diagnosed with a blood test. Each disease or condition must be individually treated, and some respond better than others. FeLV cannot be cured, but with aggressive supportive care, some cats may survive for several years beyond diagnosis. It's most important to prevent spreading FeLV to healthy cats; ask your veterinarian to advise you on your specific situation.

Vaccinations are available to help prevent the disease, but their effectiveness varies. Cats must test negative for FeLV before the vaccine can be administered. The best way to keep FeLV from infecting your cat is to prevent exposure by keeping your cat indoors and away from infected cats.

FELINE IMMUNODEFICIENCY VIRUS (FIV)

FIV, which was first identified in 1986, is similar to HIV, but each virus is species-specific: the feline AIDS virus cannot infect people, and the human virus doesn't infect cats. They both act similarly to suppress the immune system in their respective victims, though, making the cat or person susceptible to other illnesses.

Fortunately, FIV is difficult to catch. It's believed that the primary infection route is through infected saliva and that biting spreads the virus by injecting it into the victim. Cats that tend to fight—unaltered outdoor roaming felines—are therefore at highest risk.

The first symptoms of the disease—fever, swollen lymph nodes, lethargy, transient diarrhea—appear within six weeks of infection, but are often so mild they go unnoticed. Full-blown symptoms usually take three to six years to appear, which is why FIV is typically seen in cats older than five. Though they appear healthy, these cats may actually be carrying and spreading the virus.

When immunodeficiency finally hits, cats suffer persistent infections throughout their body. Symptoms can range from diarrhea and vomiting to wasting away or to claw-bed or mouth ulcers, and may mirror those of FeLV. Diagnosis is confirmed through a blood test.

There is no cure for FIV. Treatment may help keep the affected cat comfortable for a time, particularly when each problem is aggressively and promptly addressed, but FIV-infected cats usually die of these secondary illnesses. Many owners offer their pets a kinder choice by euthanizing them when they can no longer be kept comfortable.

In multi-cat homes, any FIV-positive cat should be isolated from healthy cats and kept indoors to prevent the spread of the disease. The best protection against FIV is prevention of exposure. Cats kept indoors and deprived of contact with free-roaming cats are at low risk for becoming infected.

PROTECTING PETS

Many pet diseases are incurable and deadly once the pet is infected. However, you can prevent the majority of the most serious diseases of dogs and cats by having your pet vaccinated.

Puppies and kittens are born without a mature immune system, but are protected by a "borrowed" immunity passed to them through their mother's milk. This transient immunity not only protects puppies and kittens from disease, it inactivates vaccinations. A vaccination will not become effective until the infant pet's own immunity has matured enough to take over, and the timing of this is difficult to predict. Having your puppy or kitten vaccinated one time *will not protect the pet*. Young animals must be given a series of vaccinations over the first twelve to sixteen weeks of life, so that as Mom's borrowed immunity fades, the vaccination can take over.

Adult pets also require repeated vaccinations, so that their immunity doesn't fade away. Which shots your pet needs depends on the individual's age and risk of exposure; typically, dogs and cats are revaccinated yearly, during an annual visit to the veterinarian. The vaccination schedule for dogs and cats in Appendix 3 is only a basic guide. Your veterinarian can best advise you on what protective vaccinations are most appropriate for your individual pets' situation.

CHAPTER ELEVEN

Double Trouble

In addition to the distinct conditions that specifically target dogs or cats, there are a number of health problems that affect both. There's room in this chapter only to discuss several of the most common and serious conditions.

Some common dog and cat health conditions can be treated the same way in both species. In other cases, however, even when the illness is the same, the signs may vary between the species or the treatment may be different. Understanding these differences will help keep your pets healthy.

ALLERGIES

Dogs and cats suffer from the same allergies as owners, but rather than reacting with weepy eyes and sneeze attacks, pets itch. Allergy symptoms result from an overreaction of the immune system to a substance, referred to as an allergen, that is ordinarily considered harmless.

Ongoing exposure to the allergen is required before the immune system learns to recognize it. Allergies can't be cured, but symptoms can be relieved by eliminating or reducing exposure to the allergen. It can be difficult to identify the allergen, though, and it may be impossible to avoid the irritant even once it's known.

The number one allergy in both dogs and cats is flea bite hypersensitivity. The saliva from the flea bite causes the reaction, and just one bite can trigger a week of itchy misery. Flea allergy itchiness is usually confined to the rear half of the pet, especially above the tail and down the backs of the rear legs. The excessive scratching and chewing can damage the pet's skin, or cause hair loss. Cats often develop a scabby rash called miliary dermatitis; you can feel the tiny red bumps through the fur when you pet your cat. Flea allergy is usually diagnosed by these symptoms, along with evidence of fleas. Flea control products appropriate to dogs or cats offer means of getting rid of fleas and controlling the allergy.

The second most common allergy in cats and dogs is inhalant allergy, also called atopy and often referred to as hay fever in people. Atopic pets can react to mold, pollen, dust, smoke, perfume—anything that can be inhaled. Dogs may react to the dust in cat litter; cats may react to dog fur. Feline sufferers break out in miliary dermatitis. Dogs more typically suffer front-half itching and ongoing ear infections; they rub their faces, lick and nibble their feet, and constantly scratch their neck, chest, and armpit areas.

Your veterinarian can diagnose atopy by conducting skin tests; suspect allergens are injected into the pet's skin, which will become red and swollen if that allergen is the culprit. It's difficult to protect your pet from exposure to inhaled allergens, but keeping the house as clean as possible and bathing the cat or dog regularly can help reduce dust that collects in their fur. Avoiding dusty or strongly perfumed cat litter also helps. A dietary supplement of essential fatty acids may soothe skin inflammation, while some pets respond to immunotherapy, allergy shots designed to reduce the pet's sensitivity. Immunotherapy takes months to years to become effective, and may need to continue the rest of the pet's life.

Food allergy is the third category of pet sensitivities, and is thought to be relatively rare. In dogs, the typical symptom is an intense itching all over the body. Cats suffer localized itchiness on the face and around the mouth and ears. This reaction is due to certain ingredients in pet food, not the food itself. Pets typically become allergic to proteins like beef, milk, corn, wheat, and eggs which are the most common protein ingredients in commercial foods.

Discovering which ingredients cause problems requires a weeks-long *elimination diet*. Your veterinarian diagnoses food allergy by prescribing food the pet has never eaten before, like rabbit and potato or venison and rice. If it's really a food allergy, this unique-ingredient prescription diet will relieve the itchiness. Then adding suspect ingredients to the diet again one by one until the pet again itches will identify the culprit. Once you have identified the food allergy, you can control it by feeding your pet a diet that doesn't contain that particular ingredient; look on the pet-food label's ingredient list to find an appropriate maintenance diet. It can take weeks to identify the culprits, though, and the elimination diet must be supervised by your veterinarian to prevent nutritional problems from developing.

To complicate the situation further, most pets are allergic to more than one thing. The atopic dog may also be allergic to fleas, the flea-allergic cat may be sensitive to beef. And allergies are cumulative. A pet may be able to tolerate grass pollen, but when it's combined with mold or fleas, the pet begins to itch. All pets have their own individual "itch threshold"; some may react to exposure to a single allergen, but others require two or even five before showing symptoms. You can help the allergic pet by removing one or more allergens from the equation, although it may be impossible to get rid of all culprits. If the dog or cat is allergic to house dust, pollen, and fleas, simply eliminating fleas may stop the pet from itching.

ARTHRITIS

Arthritis, an inflammation of the joints, is usually a progressive disease of old age. There are several types of arthritis, but pets most commonly suffer from osteoarthritis caused by normal wear and tear that results in painful inflammation.

Arthritis is seen most often in pets at age ten and older, and it is more common in large, heavy dogs whose extra weight places more stress on their joints. Dogs tend to suffer more joint problems than the lighter, more flexible cat.

The dog with joint pain usually limps or favors the affected area, is slow to rise after resting, and moves stiffly. Cats with the same problems mask their symptoms so well that you may not notice anything is wrong until the arthritis is quite advanced. Typically, the cat in pain simply refuses to move or does so only with great reluctance.

Canine arthritis typically appears as changes in the bone, but cats don't show the same degree of cartilage and bone degeneration as dogs and people. X-rays usually allow a vet to diagnose arthritic dogs, but cats show few signs even on X-rays and are more difficult to diagnose. Occasionally total hip or elbow replacement surgery is advocated, but pain-relieving drugs are most often the treatment of choice for pets suffering from osteoarthritis.

Never give human arthritis medications to your pets. Not only are the dosages different, but dogs and cats process drugs differently than people do and can easily be poisoned. Pain-relieving medicines like buffered aspirin may be used in dogs, but a human dose can cause stomach bleeding, or worse, so leave the dosage to a veterinarian. Aspirin, ibuprofen (Motrin and Advil), and Tylenol can all have serious or even deadly consequences if given in the wrong dose to dogs.

Cats are even more vulnerable. For a small cat, taking one adult aspirin is like a human taking thirty aspirin pills, while a single extra-strength Tylenol can kill a 10-pound cat. *Never give any medication to your pet unless instructed to do so by a veterinarian.*

Here are some things you can do at home to treat your pet's arthritis: Gently massage your pet using circular rubbing motions. Encourage the pet to exercise, so he will stay limber. Warmth works as well as anything to relieve pain; wrap a towel around a hot water bottle and place it over the painful joints. And if your pet is overweight, ask your vet for advice on slimming him down to relieve the stress on the joints.

PERIODONTAL DISEASE

Certain tooth and gum disorders are referred to as periodontal disease. About 80 percent of dogs and 70 percent of cats develop gum disease by age three. Periodontal disease is a progressive condition that worsens over time. Symptoms in both dogs and cats include yellow to brown buildup along the gum line, red inflamed gums that bleed easily, and bad breath. Mouth pain often makes the affected pet reluctant to eat.

Periodontal disease is caused when bacteria grow in food deposits that stick to teeth, producing plaque, which hardens into tartar. Gums surrounding the teeth draw away from the poisons produced by the tartar, and in dogs, this leaves deep pockets filled with plaque and pus between the gum and the tooth root. Irreversible bone damage causes teeth to loosen, fall out, or even break off. Because dogs use their mouths so much to carry and hold objects, or just for recreational chewing, broken teeth are quite common.

Cats also develop these deep pockets, but usually only around the canine teeth. More typically, gum disease in cats results in the tissue almost melting away until more and more of the tooth root is visible. Again, this causes loose teeth that can fall out.

Dogs and cats rarely suffer human-type cavities, primarily because their diet is much lower in processed sugars. But 30 percent of cats do suffer from a unique cavity called a neck lesion, which develops at the gum line where the crown and root of the tooth meet. The initial entry hole is tiny, and the decay is hidden by the gum tissue, but it eats away the inside of the tooth, leaving a hollow shell.

Pet cavities are rarely filled, because the tooth usually is too severely damaged. Extraction is the most common solution. Veterinary dentists, though, can now provide root canal work, crowns, and even orthodontic work when necessary. Treating periodontal disease consists of anesthetizing the pet and then thoroughly cleaning the teeth. Antibiotics are often necessary to fight infection.

Pets should have their teeth regularly checked and cleaned by the veterinarian, because the bacteria that cause periodontal disease not only affect the teeth but also shorten your pet's life. Chewing pumps the poison into the dog or cat's system, where it can irreparably damage the lungs, heart, liver, and kidneys. Dental care at home (see Chapter 8) will help keep your dog and cat healthy.

CANCER

Cats and dogs can suffer the same kinds of cancers that afflict people. For reasons science still can't explain, cells of the body go crazy, grow uncontrollably, and invade and replace normal tissues. When the tumor is relatively harmless, it's said to be *benign;* tumors that interfere with normal body processes are *malignant.* The cancer can be localized, but more frequently it *metastasizes,* or spreads, throughout the body.

Cancer is considered a disease of older pets; it strikes almost half of dogs and cats over the age of ten. Early detection is vital for successful treatment. Signs of cancer vary depending on the type of tumor; warning signs are listed in Table 5 in the Appendix. Most lumps and bumps you feel on your dog's skin are harmless fatty tumors or fluid-filled cysts, but 80 percent of lumps or bumps on cats are malignant.

We don't understand what causes most cancers, but there are some well-known risk factors. Too much sun can cause skin cancer, particularly in light-haired pets. Cats with white faces or ears, and dogs with white tummies, like Bull Terriers, are at highest risk for sun-induced cancer. The presence of sex hormones increases the risk of breast cancer and testicular cancer. This risk can be greatly reduced or even eliminated by neutering the pet before the onset of sexual maturity. Cats suffer from a number of virus-related cancers caused by feline leukemia virus and feline immunodeficiency virus. A very small percentage of cats develop tumors at the site where they've been vaccinated, but the risk from viral disease is much greater than that of vaccine-related sarcoma and should not discourage regular immunizations.

Dogs and cats suffer from the same types of cancer but not always with the same frequency. The most common cancer in cats is lymph gland cancers, and nearly 90 percent of these cancers are caused by FeLV infection. The lymphatic system includes the bone marrow, spleen, and lymph glands and tissues throughout the body. *Lymphoma* is the third most common cancer in dogs; the Boxer, Basset Hound, Saint Bernard, and Scottish Terrier have increased risk of developing lymphoma.

Skin cancer is the most common canine cancer and the second most common feline cancer. It's probably the least dangerous in dogs and the most malignant in cats. Skin cancer can begin as a sun-induced lesion that at first may look like a slow-to-heal sore, usually on the bridge of the nose or tip of the ear.

Breast cancer is the second leading cause of cancer in dogs, and 50 percent of these tumors are malignant. Mammary tumors are also common in cats; Siamese cats are twice as likely as other cat breeds to develop breast cancer.

Cancer of the connective tissue of the body—*fibrosarcoma*—is the third most common cancer in cats. Dogs also suffer from these tumors, which can appear anywhere on the body. Bone cancer, or *osteosarcoma,* is one of the more common cancers in dogs, especially the giant breeds. It's less common in cats, but it does occur. A wide variety of other cancers—in any part of the body, from head to tail—also affect dogs and cats.

Diagnosis of the specific cancer is made by microscopic examination of the tumor cells. Prognosis depends on the type of cancer and how advanced it is at the time of diagnosis. Some cancers can be cured when caught early. Treatment also depends on the type of cancer and the location of the tumor.

The same three types of cancer treatment used in people also apply to dogs and cats. Surgery is the treatment of choice in veterinary cancer therapy. When the location or invasiveness of the tumor makes surgery a poor choice, chemotherapy may be used. Unlike human patients, cats and dogs don't typically suffer side effects from chemotherapy; they don't lose their coat, and they don't suffer the nausea that people do. Radiation therapy is also used on pet cancers that are difficult to remove surgically; it is most effective on bone and skin cancers that grow very quickly.

These therapies used alone or in combination may help prolong the pet's life even when a cure isn't possible.

INTESTINAL PARASITES

COCCIDIOSIS is caused by a protozoan that attack the lining of the intestine. Pets become infected by swallowing infectious protozoan, which is found in the soil and in the stool of other pets and of wild rodents. Adult cats and dogs may harbor this parasite, but puppies and kittens are more severely affected. Infected pets pass a loose stool that contains mucus and blood, and this

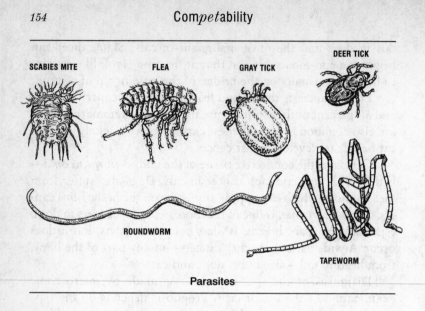

SCABIES MITE   FLEA   GRAY TICK   DEER TICK

ROUNDWORM

TAPEWORM

Parasites

sign may come and go. Diagnosis is made by microscopic examination of the stool. Sulfa-type drugs are effective against this parasite. Some pets may require hospitalization to reverse dehydration caused by the diarrhea.

GIARDIASIS is caused by another protozoan, which lives in the small intestine and interferes with the pet's digestion. Signs are similar to those of coccidiosis, but many dogs and cats don't display any signs. However, *Giardia* live in the environment and can infect the water supply and cause diarrhea in humans. It's hard to find this organism even with a microscope. Pets suspected of carrying these protozoans are treated with a drug called metronidazole, which kills the parasite.

HOOKWORMS are an intestinal parasite common in dogs and less common in cats. The tiny worms take bites out of the small intestine and live on the pet's blood. Some pets contract the condition by swallowing infective larvae or eating an infected mouse or cockroach; others are infected when the larvae penetrate their skin. Puppies (but not kittens) can be infected by their mother before they're born, but most puppy infections happen when they swallow their mother's infected milk. Hookworm infestation causes anemia from blood loss and diarrhea. In dogs and especially puppies (but rarely cats), the stool is bloody, deep red, or black and tarry. Hookworms can cause sudden collapse and death in very young pets. Diagnosis is made by finding the eggs during microscopic examination of the stool. A liquid oral medication called Nemex (pyrantel pamoate) is effective in killing the worms.

ROUNDWORMS may be the most common intestinal parasite in puppies and kittens; they look like masses of spaghetti when passed in the stool or vomited. Puppies are often born with them or get them through Mom's milk; kittens typically are infected from nursing their mother. Pets can also pick up roundworms in the environment or by eating rodents. Though adult pets don't usually suffer problems from these parasites, a large number of roundworms can lead to death in young pets. Diagnosis is made by finding the microscopic eggs or the adult worms in the pet's stool. Affected pets often have a full, potbellied look, dull fur, and sometimes diarrhea or mucus in the stool. The same medication used for hookworms is effective against roundworms, and Nemex is safe to use in three- to four-week-old pets.

TAPEWORMS are segmented intestinal parasites that can reach 2 feet in length. Cats and dogs most commonly contract tapeworms when they ingest infected fleas, but they can also get them from eating infested rodents. Tapeworms can interfere with digestion and, in large numbers, may block the intestines. Diagnosis is made by finding tiny white ricelike segments in the stool or stuck to the hair near the pet's tail. Droncit (praziquantel) is an effective medication given as pills or injections, but the best prevention is eradicating fleas.

WHIPWORMS are contracted from the environment, and live in the pet's large intestine. They most often affect dogs; cats are very rarely infested. These parasites feed on blood and, in small numbers, cause few signs. A heavy infestation, however, results in diarrhea, anemia, and weight loss. Diagnosis is made by finding eggs during microscopic examination of the dog's stool. Effective medications are available, but dogs are often reinfected because of soil contaminated with infected eggs.

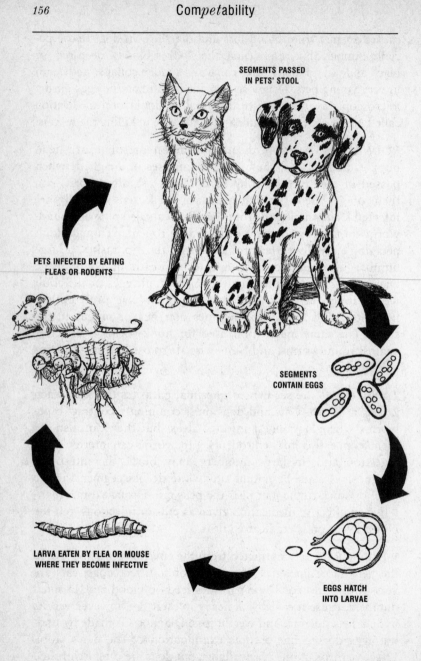

SEGMENTS PASSED IN PETS' STOOL

PETS INFECTED BY EATING FLEAS OR RODENTS

SEGMENTS CONTAIN EGGS

LARVA EATEN BY FLEA OR MOUSE WHERE THEY BECOME INFECTIVE

EGGS HATCH INTO LARVAE

Tapeworm life cycle

Good hygiene goes a long way toward preventing intestinal parasites in cats and dogs. Keep the litter box clean, and pick up the yard after your dog.

EXTERNAL PARASITES

FLEAS are the most common external parasite of dogs and cats. Recognizing and eliminating flea infestation is discussed in Chapter 8.

CUTEREBRA is a fly larva that commonly affects rodents. Dogs and cats contract this parasite by frequenting mouse and rabbit runs. Cuterebra enters the pet's body through the nose or mouth, then migrates and ends up in a pocket under the skin. The site, usually on the neck or chest, will swell as the larva grows and matures for up to a month. The swelling may resemble an abscess and usually has a central air hole that may drain blood-tinged fluid. Though Cuterebra rarely cause the pet distress, the cysts can become infected. They must be removed surgically by a veterinarian; crushing the parasite may poison the pet and cause a life-threatening reaction. Left alone, the spine-covered brown larva reaches an inch and a half in length before breaking free of the skin.

EAR MITES, which are related to spiders, live on the surface of the ear and in the ear canal, where they pierce the skin and drink lymph. The dog or cat infested with these creepy-crawlies will suffer an itch that can't be scratched. Signs include a dark waxy debris inside the ears and excessive head-shaking and ear-scratching. The inflammation of the ears can develop into infection.

Diagnosis is made by locating the mite during microscopic examination of ear debris. These bugs are extremely contagious; if one pet in the house has them, all the pets—cats, dogs, ferrets, rabbits—should be treated. Cleaning out the ears and applying a veterinary-prescribed insecticide to kill the mites is the usual treatment. At times the dog or cat's ears are so sore that the pet must be anesthetized during treatment. Occasionally an injectable medication called ivermectin may be used.

TICKS are blood-sucking parasites related to spiders. More than 650 kinds of ticks can affect dogs and cats; pets pick them up simply by walking through the grass. Most ticks are brown to gray with hard, flat, oval bodies that grow plump like tiny blood-filled balloons when attached to a pet and feeding on its blood. Tick bites can cause sores, and massive infestations can result in anemia; more importantly, ticks carry a number of diseases—like Lyme disease—that cause illness and sometimes death in pets and people (decribed in Appendix 3).

In most instances, the tick must feed for twelve to twenty-four hours before any organisms will be transmitted to the host. Therefore, removing ticks from your pet as soon as possible will reduce the chance of disease. Ticks don't hop off one host and onto another, which means people rarely get tick-borne diseases from their pets. Removing ticks with your bare hands does expose you to disease, however, so wear gloves and use tweezers to remove ticks. Some flea preparations are also effective against ticks. Although cats can also be affected, dogs are usually harder hit by this parasite because cats tend to groom them away before disease can be transmitted.

RINGWORM

Ringworm is a fungal infection of the hair, nails, and skin that can affect dogs, cats, and people. It's called ringworm because in people the sores grow outward in rings. In dogs and cats, however, the condition often mimics any number of other skin diseases. Bald patches are the most common sign, and puppies and kittens are most often affected.

Pets can contract this condition from infected soil. Ringworm is quite contagious; you can give it to your dog or cat, and your pets can give it to one an other or to you. Infected pets should be isolated to prevent the spread of the infection. Pets, especially cats, can sometimes carry the fungus and spread the infection to other pets without showing signs themselves.

Diagnosis is based on visible symptoms and on laboratory tests. Pets tend to heal in 60 to 100 days without treatment. To speed recovery, an oral medicine called griseofulvin may be used, sometimes along with a topical treatment like a lime-sulfur dip.

A vaccine is also available for the treatment of ringworm; ask your veterinarian if it's appropriate for your pet.

Ringworm fungus can live in the environment for well over a year and can continuously reinfect your pets. The most effective environmental treatment consists of daily cleaning of all surfaces using a solution of one part bleach to ten parts water. Also vacuum every day, seal the used vacuum bags in plastic, and remove them from the house.

DIABETES

Diabetes mellitus results when the pancreas produces too little insulin, the hormone that helps move sugar into the cells, where it is used to create energy. When there's not enough insulin, the body starves. The diabetic pet loses weight, even as she eats more and more food.

The sugar that can't be used builds up in the body and is eliminated by the kidneys. Sugar in the urine pulls more water out of the body, which makes the dog or cat very thirsty. Diabetic pets drink lots of water and urinate a great deal more than is normal.

Since the body can't use sugar for energy, it eventually begins to burn its own fat and muscle tissue. The resulting by-products are a type of acid called ketone bodies, which in excess numbers can kill the pet. Signs of this condition, called *ketoacidosis,* include labored rapid breathing and breath that smells like nail-polish remover. Without treatment, the diabetic dog or cat will die.

Diagnosis is based on the visible signs of disease, along with blood and urine tests. Excess sugar in the urine is a strong indication of diabetes.

This disease cannot be cured, but it can usually be controlled. Excess fat tends to inhibit the effect of insulin, so slimming down the fat cat or dog often improves the condition. Most diabetic pets require insulin injections, the dosage and timing of which must be determined by the veterinarian.

Owners can learn to give insulin to a diabetic pet. It's very important that meals and exercise for the pet remain constant, because unexpected exercise or an unauthorized snack can throw off the amount of insulin that's needed. Too much or too little insulin can be devastating.

Insulin coma results when the pet doesn't get enough insulin. Too much results in hypoglycemia, with the pet becoming disoriented and shaky, or even suffering convulsions or coma. Both are emergencies, and you must seek the help of a veterinarian immediately if your pet is to survive.

HEART DISEASE

Acquired valvular heart disease is a disease of old age and is the most common form of heart disease in the dog. The heart valves begin to wear out and leak blood backward instead of pumping it all forward. This puts extra strain on the heart muscle.

About one-third of all dogs over the age of twelve are affected, and the earliest sign is a harsh, dry cough that frequently occurs at night or following exercise. Other signs include labored breathing, weakness, fainting, and edema—the collection of fluid in the tissues which may cause the legs or the abdomen to swell.

Diagnosis is made using X-rays, ultrasound, and electrocardiograms that pick up irregular heart rhythms. Drugs are available that help improve the heart's performance and reduce fluid accumulation. With medication a dog often remains comfortable for the rest of his life.

The most common type of heart disease in cats is cardiomyopathy. In this disease it's the heart muscle that causes problems. Cardiomyopathy can affect a cat at any age, and some forms may be inherited.

Cats with heart disease almost never cough and often hide signs until the disease is quite advanced. Labored breathing, even during rest, is the most common sign. Like dogs, cats may suffer edema and weakness or fainting spells. Cats with cardiomyopathy also may suffer sudden hind limb pain or paralysis caused by blood clots from the damaged heart.

The same diagnostic tests and many of the same drugs are used in both cats and dogs. "Clot-busting" drugs or sometimes surgery may be required to relieve the paralysis. If dilated cardiomyopathy is due to taurine deficiency, correcting the diet may cure the disease. For the most part, however, once signs of feline heart disease are seen, most cats die within a few months.

HEARTWORM

Heartworm disease is caused by a parasite transmitted by mosquitoes. Adult worms live in the pulmonary arteries and heart chambers, and eventually compromise the effectiveness of this organ. Heartworms are primarily a threat to dogs, but they can also attack cats.

Pets get this disease when they are bitten by a mosquito carrying the infectious stage of the parasite. The immature heartworms burrow into the host's body, going through several molts as they grow. In two to four months, they reach a vein and are carried to the pulmonary arteries that lead from the heart to the lungs. There they mature, and when their numbers are too great, they spill over into the right side of the heart. Once sexually mature, the adult worms mate and give birth to baby worms called microfilariae, which live in the circulating bloodstream. The microfilariae are then swallowed by subsequent mosquitoes when they feed, and they mature inside the mosquito to the infective stage. The cycle is complete in six to seven months.

It's not uncommon for infected dogs to carry hundreds of worms. Heartworm disease in dogs is a chronic condition. Worms live in the dog for up to five years, and symptoms grow worse over time. Common signs are coughing, shortness of breath, and a reluctance to exercise—dogs may even faint after exertion. Eventually the dog becomes weak, listless, loses weight, and may cough up blood. Severe signs of late-stage disease are heart failure, including labored breathing and edema. The condition may result in sudden collapse and death.

Infected cats may not show any symptoms at all, or they may suffer sudden breathing difficulty and die within minutes. Dogs often live with many worms, but it takes only one worm to cause symptoms in a cat, and two worms can kill. And while dogs tend to develop signs of heart failure, cats don't. Instead, cats suffer breathing problems similar to asthma; they sometimes cough, and they may vomit for no apparent reason. Cats with heart disease rarely cough, so coughing can be an indication of heartworm infection. They also lose weight, suffer weakness, and may suddenly collapse.

Heartworm disease is diagnosed in dogs by finding microfilariae in the bloodstream. But cats almost never develop baby worms because they rarely harbor enough worms to reproduce. Cats can be infected with heartworms only when there are infected dogs present to supply mosquitoes with the microfilariae. X-rays, echocardiography, and a combination of blood-screening techniques are used to diagnose the condition in cats.

Once diagnosed, dogs can be treated with injections of a drug called thiacetarsamide, which kills the adult worms in the heart. Then the dog must rest for several weeks until the dead worms are absorbed by the body; sudden exertion could set a mass of worm debris in motion, and this could cause a life-threatening blockage, or *embolism*. After three to six weeks the dog is treated with medicine to kill the microfilariae that still circulate in the bloodstream.

Unfortunately, cats have a much greater chance of embolism, and treatment with thiacetarsamide often kills the cat as well as the worms. Heartworm disease in cats is generally treated only with supportive care that attempts to soothe the cat's symptoms, in the hope that the cat will survive the infection on her own.

It is much easier to prevent heartworm disease than to diagnose, treat, and cure it once infection is present. Several preventive medications have been available for dogs for many years. In January 1997 the first feline heartworm preventive was approved. Ask your veterinarian to recommend an appropriate heartworm prevention regimen for your dog and cat.

KIDNEY DISEASE

Kidneys, which filter toxins and waste from blood, can be damaged when subjected to infections or poisons like antifreeze or from drug toxicities like Tylenol. More commonly, the kidneys simply wear out and become less efficient as the dog or cat ages. Most dogs over the age of eight, and up to 30 percent of cats over the age of fifteen suffer some degree of kidney damage.

But dog and cat kidneys are able to continue working even when damaged, and problems are often masked for quite some time. Signs of disease may not show until 70 percent of function is gone, and pet owners may not notice that anything is wrong until kidney disease is quite advanced. Left untreated, the affected cat or dog will fall into a coma and die.

Typical signs are increased thirst and urination due to the inability of the kidneys to concentrate urine. The pet drinks more to compensate for increased water loss, drinking more water increases urination, and a vicious cycle ensues. Affected pets will often drink from the toilet bowl, the fish tank, or the sink. Accidents happen when pets can't reach the litter box or yard in time. Later symptoms include loss of appetite and weight loss, weakness, depression, vomiting, and diarrhea or constipation. Sores appear on the tongue and in the mouth, along with a brownish discoloration on the tongue and breath that smells like ammonia.

The diagnosis is based on signs and on blood and urine tests. With treatment, many dogs and cats can live comfortably for several years after diagnosis. Medications help normalize the blood, and a special high-quality diet with reduced protein and phosphorus will help lessen the strain on the pet's kidneys. Lots of fresh water should be available at all times. In a small percentage of cases, especially in cats, a kidney transplant is a possibility.

Dogs and cats approaching middle age should be screened for kidney disease whether they're showing signs or not. Early detection and appropriate treatment are the best ways to keep your dog and cat living healthy into old age.

LOWER URINARY TRACT DISEASES

Both dogs and cats suffer from lower urinary tract disorders. Cats can be affected by a group of problems collectively referred to as feline lower urinary tract disease (FLUTD), which in the past was called feline urologic disease or FUS.

Three broad types of problems are considered typical of the syndrome in both dogs and cats. The first is *cystitis,* inflammation of the urinary bladder. In dogs, cystitis is almost always caused by a bacterial infection and is treated with an antibiotic. In cats, the cause usually isn't known, but the condition is aggravated by stress.

The second problem is the formation of urinary stones, mineral crystals that range from microscopic to the size of a Ping-Pong ball. People tend to form stones in the kidneys, but the bladder is the typical location for dogs and cats. Infections commonly cause canine bladder stones, while diet appears to influence the condition in cats. There's an inherited tendency in dogs—the Pekingese, Dachshund, Cocker Spaniel, and Dalmatian are at highest risk— and there may be a genetic influence in cats, but this hasn't been determined. Because of the dog's greater size, canine bladder stones tend to be larger and often require surgical removal. Feline stones more typically are the size of a grain of sand or even smaller. A special diet may dissolve certain kinds of canine or feline bladder stones. Stones irritate the lining of the urinary tract and may block the passage of urine.

Blockage is a life-threatening emergency that occurs when the passage of urine is cut off. In dogs, the most common cause of urinary blockage is the presence of stones in the bladder or urethra. Cats, though, usually suffer blockage when a pastelike material, sometimes mixed with sandlike crystals, plugs the urethral opening. The cause of feline urethral plugs is still being investigated.

Urinary blockage is excruciating for the pet. The bladder expands with urine, which has no means of escape and which may back up into the kidneys. Blockage is an emergency that needs immediate veterinary attention: within seventy-two hours of complete blockage, the pet will die.

The signs of lower urinary tract problems can be any one or a combination of the following: a break in house-training, dribbling urine, spending lots of time in the litter box or out in the yard straining with little result, bloody urine or urine with a strong ammonia smell, crying during urination, or excessive licking at the genitals. Dogs of either sex may display an odd splay-legged posture during painful urination, and partial obstruction may be indicated by a weak, splattery stream of urine even when the dog is not in distress. Among cats it's the males that tend to be blocked, because of their narrower urethral opening. Diagnosis is based on symptoms and on analysis of the pet's urine.

The veterinarian usually unblocks the pet by using a catheter and then flushing the crystals and paste plugs from the system. If a catheter won't work, a needle can be inserted through the abdomen into the bladder to drain away the urine.

Hospitalization for up to a week is often required to stabilize the pet.

There is no way to predict which pets may suffer from lower urinary tract disease or to prevent the condition from arising. But once a pet has suffered an episode, the veterinarian may be able to offer some management options, depending on the specific problems.

RABIES

Rabies is a deadly disease that can affect warm-blooded animals, including dogs, cats, and people. The virus attacks the brain and causes neurological disorders, and once symptoms appear, the disease is always fatal. In the United States, it's primarily a disease of wild animals, but the virus can easily spill over into our pet population from infected raccoons, coyotes, foxes, bats, or other wild creatures. Usually the disease is transmitted by a bite.

Signs of disease can develop fourteen days to twenty-four months following the bite, but they most typically appear within three to eight weeks. Symptoms are behavior changes; animals usually stop eating and drinking, and seek solitude. Then they either become vicious or show signs of paralysis.

In the first form of rabies, often called *dumb rabies,* the dog or cat acts depressed and sick. Paralysis of the throat and jaw muscles, drooling, and difficulty swallowing often follow, as if the pet has something stuck in its throat. These animals are completely insensitive to pain, and usually become comatose and die three to ten days after the first symptoms appear.

The second form of the disease is called *furious rabies* and is typified by classic mad dog symptoms. Such animals are extremely vicious and violent, snap and bite at real or imaginary objects, and may roam for miles attacking anything in their path. They lose all fear of natural enemies, commonly chew or swallow foreign objects, and tend to have a blank, spooky, or anxious look. Cats most often suffer this form, and an affected feline will vocalize a great deal. The cat may also have a wobbly or collapsing gait affecting the rear legs. Paralysis becomes progressively worse until death occurs four to seven days after symptoms are first seen.

Diagnosis of rabies is based on symptoms, but can be confirmed only by microscopic examination of the brain tissue. Suspect animals are euthanized so they can be tested.

Because of the human risk factor, many states require that dogs and cats be vaccinated for rabies. Recently, the incidence of rabies has become much higher in pet cats than in pet dogs, because fewer owners have their cats vaccinated.

If your pet is exposed to rabies—in other words, if it is bitten by a suspect animal—consult your veterinarian immediately. Rules regarding rabies vary from state to state. When the pet isn't current on vaccinations, a six-month quarantine may be enforced, and only when signs don't develop will the pet be vaccinated and released back into your care. Pets that have been vaccinated and then bitten are usually immediately revaccinated, with strict owner control and observation for no less than forty-five days.

Have both your cats and your dogs vaccinated against rabies to protect them and yourself. Some vaccines protect pets for one year; others give three years of protection. Each state has its own requirements, so ask your veterinarian about the vaccination schedule appropriate for your pets.

PART FOUR

Canine Culture and Feline Language

CHAPTER TWELVE

The Pack Mentality
versus the Despot

The differences between dogs and cats are greater than their similarities in nearly every way. Nowhere is this more apparent than in the way they relate to others of their kind, to other animals, and to people. These behavior patterns are what characterize the canine and feline social structures.

Dogs and cats live by a protocol that defines proper etiquette for each species as they relate to one another. This understanding of common rules of behavior is a built-in survival mechanism shared with their wild cousins.

Social groups form to present a united front toward outside adversaries. They may hunt together, protect the nest and young, or defend their territory from intruders, and this means that individuals must work toward a common goal. Yet in any gathering of creatures—cat, dog, human, whatever—there are inevitably differences of opinion. The greater the number of individuals making up the group, the more conflicts there will be.

When disputes arise, a mechanism must be in place to settle the matter quickly and without permanent damage to the group. A knockdown, to-the-death altercation is not beneficial; eventually there'd be nobody left, and a group of one is no group at all. Dogs and cats have developed unique social systems to address these situations.

Canine culture is founded on a basic pack mentality which in many ways mirrors that of human society. Cat culture, on the other hand, is marked by a fluid yet despotic rule, a notion foreign to people and dogs. When a household includes creatures from these very different worlds, there's likely to be a culture clash. It is up to you, the pet owner, to be the mediator between the two. If there is to be peace in your home, you must be the despot, and your first step is to understand the mentality of both pets.

LEADER OF THE PACK

The dog's social structure, like that of its wolf ancestors, is based on a hierarchy of dominant and submissive individuals. Where an individual falls in this canine pecking order depends on a number of factors, all interrelated. But the pet owner had better be at the top of the heap.

First, though, let's get something straight: Dominance does not mean aggressiveness, and neither does submission necessarily mean fearfulness. One does not need to be a bully to be in charge. Dogs know this and act accordingly.

In fact, the dominant dog is so secure in his place that he has nothing to prove and rarely needs to fight or argue with subordinates. Other dogs give way naturally, without argument, and accept that this is the way things should be. In the same way, an owner who knows the correct way to lead has no need to use bullying tactics. Dogs in your household will want to please you because you are the leader. All you have to do is remind Poochie who's the boss and instruct him how to please you.

Personality probably has the greatest influence on canine social status. Some dogs are just naturally bolder than others, while some are timid. Certain breeds and families of dogs tend toward one extreme or another, but socialization is the biggest influence on canine personality. As discussed previously, puppies who experience novel situations early in life are better prepared for the unexpected and will usually be less timid as adults.

Canine size would seem to dictate dominance to a great extent, but anyone who has ever lived with a Chihuahua knows this isn't necessarily so. It's not the size of the package, but what's inside that's important.

The balance of power depends most upon interaction among specific members of a social group. Territorial claims also change status; one dog may have the most clout in the house while another rules the backyard. Social ranking becomes even more complicated as the number of individuals in the pack increases.

Fortunately, dogs are usually quite civilized and rarely settle disputes of social rank through violent means. Instead of out-and-out wrangling, dogs have developed an intricate system of visual and verbal signals, which they use to resolve all kinds of doggy dilemmas. (Canine communication will be explored in detail in Chapter 13.)

CANINE POKER

Sorting out canine social status is a lot like playing cards. Each dog plays the hand he or she has been dealt. When the dog isn't satisfied with the cards, or fears they're not up to snuff, he may attempt to bluff to win the pot.

What are winning cards? Sexual status is a big one. Generally speaking, an intact animal will hold a position of dominance over one that's been neutered. Unless you're a professional breeder, there's really no good reason for keeping a dog intact, male or female. Neutering all of your pets will help even the playing field, and solve many problems before they begin.

Age is another important factor, particularly as it relates to other animals. Adult dogs tend to be dominant over puppies and juvenile animals. And dogs in their prime generally outrank geriatric dogs. Dogs of the same age have no clear-cut advantage over one another. Adolescent dogs of about a year old may try to outbluff the dominant dog, and this can cause fireworks— usually more noise than anything else—until the top dog is definitively established.

Health status is another valuable card. A healthy subordinate will recognize that a sick leader doesn't stand a chance of enforcing his dominance and may make a move to usurp the sick dog's position.

Finally, the home-turf advantage is incredibly important. The dog on his own territory can tell a trespasser to hit the road—and the stranger will do so. His acquiescence is simply canine etiquette; dogs recognize that the owner of the property is king of that territory. When on his own territory a dog is dominant, but in a stranger's territory, he becomes subordinate to the owner of that territory. That's why the tiny Chihuahua can drive away the trespassing Great Dane.

Territorial rights also extend to a dog's personal space. People share this reluctance to stand too close to others, particularly strangers. The comfort zone is different from person to person and from dog to dog, and varies between canine breeds just as it does in human cultures. Some people—and some dogs—are more tolerant than others of close encounters, but crowded conditions will bring out the worst in most of us.

But just as we say "pardon me" out of respect to those we inadvertently bump into in the supermarket, dogs do their best to respect one another's comfort zone. The leader of the pack, though, will have the greatest latitude in being able to encroach on the comfort zone of others.

Although one dog may seem to hold all the right cards, he may not always win the dominant position, particularly if an adversary knows how to bluff. The older dog may be put in his place by a Young Turk who can put on a good show and wear the old-timer down. And an extroverted in-your-face puppy may easily buffalo a clueless adult dog who has never before experienced a canine social relationship.

DOGGY FAIR PLAY

Dogs don't have to fight to the death to establish who the top dog is. They use signals not only to communicate dominance but also to cry uncle. They'll usually recognize a subordinate's plea for mercy and pull back from full-blown aggression once their superiority has been acknowledged.

Not every dog aspires to being leader of the pack; most are satisfied just with being a member. Ultimately for dogs, the group is more important than the individual.

Dogs support their positions within the pack with ritualized displays of submission to those in a superior position. The blatant posturing of doggy greetings and signs of respect serve to reinforce the relationship between individuals. Squabbles for position occur only when there is no clear leadership. And once every pet knows its place in the scheme of things, the kingdom will remain at peace.

THE FELINE DESPOT

The cat's social structure, like that of the dog, is based on dominant and subordinate individuals. But where the dog embraces a linear system of stairstep ranking, top to bottom, the feline social arrangement consists of a pedestal mind-set. One dominant cat perches above the others, while those below are all on the same subordinate level. Subordinate cats do not act like submissive dogs, but are instead motivated by defensiveness or even avoidance.

This despotic system makes sense when you consider the cat's self-sufficient style of living. Wildcats hunt alone and come together only to breed and raise kittens. When vying for a female's favor, only one tomcat needs to win; being number two, three, or whatever doesn't really matter to the losing males, because there's no reason for them to hang around or get along with the winner. And when the queen gives birth, she's the boss to her kittens, and they're all on one level below her. When the kittens mature, they head off on their own.

In canine society, when the number one dog is absent, the number two dog naturally steps up and becomes leader of the pack. But in the cat's despotic world, no specific cat is in line for the crown; a tumble from the pedestal results in a free-for-all until a new king or queen cat is crowned.

In studies of farm cats with a ready food source, feline social groups appear to be structured like lion society. Related adult females with overlapping territories share a core territory where individuals eat and sleep together and collectively rear kittens born to the group. One cat in the group rarely enjoys total dominance, and the ranking order among females is fluid and based primarily on their roles as mothers. Having kittens raises the mother's social status; the cat with the greatest number of litters attains the highest rank. The group bands together to defend territory from strange females and recruits new members from among the maturing female kittens within their own ranks.

The male cats are more loosely attached to these groups and may range between several female groups that are in close proximity to one another. The availability of females rather than food determines the male cat's territorial range. Groups of tomcats that know one another may hang out in a kind of loosely organized brotherhood, with ranking determined through highly ritualized duels. These face-offs rarely cause injury. Once rank is established, male cats don't need to fight unless challenged by a younger wanna-be or faced by a strange male. Fights with unknown males who don't belong to the club can turn serious, though, and may result in injury to both parties.

The territorial range of outdoor cat societies can encompass acres or even miles. Male cat ranges are typically ten times as large as a female's territory and often overlap the ranges of other cats. This is possible because cats utilize a kind of time-share policy to avoid face-to-face encounters when in foreign territory.

The same principle applies to house cats. The territory is compressed, and the house itself becomes the extent of the cat's range. The yard viewed from the windows is also considered cat property, even if Kitty never sets foot off the carpet. When there is more than one cat in the house, a forced social group emerges, and the cats adapt to the situation.

KITTY POKER

Many of the same cards that influence canine dominance and submission are important in feline social stature as well. Sexual status also plays a major role in feline communities. Intact males and females wield more power than neutered ones, and the queen with kittens carries the most clout of all. For all the reasons previously stated, neutering your pets simplifies a great many things, especially com*pet*ability issues.

The cats' sex may also influence how well they interact. But after they are neutered, personalities tend to matter more than gender. Male cats, however, usually require more territory than females, whether they're neutered or not, and this may be a consideration when the pets need to be kept indoors.

Personality, age, and health status also influence feline social standing. The brash, in-your-face cat typically has a better chance of ruling the roost than the timid shrinking violet. Ill cats are easy targets for healthy ones. Mature cats typically rule over youngsters, and cats in their prime tend to dominate geriatric felines.

Of course, there are always exceptions. Callie was six years old and had always been an only cat when suddenly a three-week-old orphan kitten joined the family. Callie had never had to jockey for position and didn't know what to do when Katy began—as kittens do—using her as a punching bag, tag partner, and general butt of kitten pranks. Callie, despite her seniority, simply hid.

More typically, one cat will emerge in the house as the dominant operative, with the others giving way to her whims. And, like dogs, cats have their own way of sorting out their differences and establishing social position. Feline communication will be discussed further, along with dog dialogue, in Chapter 13.

Cats are masters at the bluff. Fur rarely flies in feline face-offs; instead, a great deal of posturing takes place. It's the feline equivalent of playing chicken; whichever cat turns tail and runs, unable to take the pressure, loses furry face—and status.

Feline communication is particularly important because the house cat's range is so limited. The smallest natural range of a free-roaming cat is still far larger than the typical house. Nearly all dogs are given yard privileges, but the exclusively indoor cat must settle for the owner's home.

Property means status to the cat, and even the most submissive feline must feel she "owns" something. When there is more than one cat in the house, property is divided up, with the most dominant cat taking over the prime real estate. In other words, just because one cat is dominant doesn't mean the others can't have their own tiny piece of the pie—as long as the dominant kitty doesn't decide he or she wants it.

Actually this system is quite democratic in a catty sort of way. The most dominant cat may "own" the first floor, while the second floor of the house "belongs" to another cat. Each cat defends her property against interlopers. The more cats there are, the greater the difficulty of dividing everything up. Generally speaking, as long as each cat has a room of her own, they tend to adjust to the situation—a four-bedroom house can accommodate four cats comfortably. But when there's not enough space to go around, all of them get their tails in a twist.

Cats capitalize on vertical space. Very literally, the top cat will grab the highest and best lookout for herself. The top of the television or refrigerator is prime feline real estate.

Cats also have individual comfort zones, like dogs, and their tolerance varies from individual to individual. A cat may happily sleep with one feline buddy but refuse to endure another cat in the same room with her.

Unlike dogs, who usually settle down once they know their place, cats are less forgiving. The elaborate canine ceremonial obeisance to superiors doesn't exist in feline society, because every cat believes in her heart that she's a queen just waiting to be crowned. Many times a subordinate feline will look the other way and pretend not to see rather than submit to a dominant cat.

And when two cats simply can't agree as to which should rule, they often simply ignore each other. Instead of competing for a given resource, they time-share. This makes it difficult to tell who's the top cat in a multi-cat home.

Nonetheless, most house cats get along well with one another, particularly when all are neutered and have been properly introduced. Cats that were raised in a litter of four or more kittens that remained together during the important socialization period usually get along well with other cats. Oftentimes the feline dance of dominance is so subtle that only the cats realize anything has occurred. Cats are incredibly flexible; left to their own devices, most cats work out their differences and live peaceably together.

ALL IN THE FAMILY

What happens when these two very different social systems come together? In many ways, the feline and canine cultures seem to complement each other.

Dogs and cats who have been socialized to each other early in life accept one another's foibles quite willingly. Now, don't misunderstand; they know they're different from each other, but they've learned to recognize each other individually as part of their personal group.

Consider that the dog is a pack animal who's totally satisfied as long as he knows his place in the family. The unwritten rules of the pack require him to follow the leader; he doesn't care who it is, just as long as there's a designated leader for him to follow.

As the despot in residence, the cat is happy to assume a position of authority. Kitty doesn't particularly care who she's bossing around, as long as she ends up occupying the prime real estate, the more elevated the better. Dogs can't climb, so the cat is already at an advantage here.

Dogs and cats will often accept each other in the same household as a matter of course. Occasionally, however, a bit of maneuvering goes on, and the waters are tested before peace reigns. The cat doesn't always end up number one in the household. There are dominant dogs who demand respect, but of course cats rarely offer anything on demand. Instead, Kitty will most likely opt for avoidance, which results in the dog time-sharing at the cat's whim—whether he knows it or not.

Let your pets sort out their hierarchy themselves. One of them is going to come out on top, and that's as it should be. Human rules and your sense of fair play cannot and should not figure in. Interference will only prolong the jockeying for position and make all of you miserable.

That's not to say bloodshed should be allowed. More often than not, the pets will engage in one or more rounds of bluffing, with much posturing and loud vocalizations. Unless a pitched battle seems imminent, leave them alone. (See Chapter 15 for specific tactics for safely introducing new pets to each other.)

Remember that each pet wants very different things out of life. Dogs want to belong to a family with a leader they can properly adore. Cats want control over as much territory as possible. Different perspectives but the same goal. The most important member of your pet's family group is you. You are the dog's beloved leader, and you are the most important element of your cat's territory.

That's a lot of responsibility. One of the most important ways you can show your leadership and promote com*pet*ability in your home is to support the social standing of your pets. In other words, don't champion the underdog—or undercat. This holds true whether the participants are two dogs, two cats, or a dog and a cat. Giving the same amount of attention to a clearly subordinate pet as to the dominant one risks putting King Pet's nose out of joint. When that happens, King Pet must reinforce his own status by figuratively kicking the other pet's lowly tail.

If Kitty chases Poochie off the bed, don't invite the dog back up and try to make them share the covers. If Poochie jumps on your lap to keep the cat away, give the cat some quality time when Poochie is outside or otherwise engaged—don't punish the dog for wanting to adore you. If you're not careful, your misguided sense of fair play may actually cause more trouble between the two.

Remember that your home should be a peaceable *kingdom,* not a democracy. You must rule with authority to keep all the subjects happy. An effective leader is a wise leader. To best understand your pets, you must learn what they're saying. Otherwise, misunderstandings are inevitable. And to get along in your kingdom, you and your pets must be bilingual.

CHAPTER THIRTEEN

Say What?

The languages of dogs and cats are no less intricate than our own. In human communication the emphasis is on vocalization where words convey meaning and the tone of voice implies emotional intent. Body language, as expressed in the speaker's posture and facial expression, transmits subtle, even subliminal, messages.

Dog and cat communication also employs vocalization. Barks, whimpers, meows, and chirps all have meaning. But pet communication relies more on posture, body position, facial expression, and movement of legs, tail, and even fur. In addition, dogs and cats include visual and olfactory signposts in their vocabulary in much the way we do the written word. They also communicate through touch.

Vocalization permits pets to communicate over long distances or in situations where vision is impaired—at night, for instance. It not only communicates to pack members but also alerts prey and other predators. Silent communication, on the other hand, is in many ways safer and can be more intense. A cat or dog is able to sustain a growl for only one breath at a time, but a silent stare or body posture can be held indefinitely. And a scented message left behind on a prominent landmark will last for days without the author even needing to be present.

Living together in harmony requires the owner to comprehend both pets' languages. While humans can't begin to understand the subtleties of scent communication, we are able to recognize many visual and vocal cues.

Equally important, pets must understand each other. Signals are not always clear, particularly in breeds whose facial expressions are hidden by lots of fur, pendulous, folded, or cropped ears, or a tail that is docked or varies from the archetypical tail.

More often, signals are clear but are misinterpreted. Dogs and cats have some vocabulary in common, but many signals have different or even opposite meanings. Misunderstandings between dogs and cats often stem from this language barrier.

HOWLS AND PURRS

Although vocalization is a small part of your pets' communication, all dogs and cats are vocal. How mouthy they are varies from individual to individual and occasionally from breed to breed. For instance, the Siamese cat and related breeds are known to be talkative. They have distinctive, compelling voices, which they use a great deal. Some dogs, particularly northern breeds like the Alaskan Malamute, indulge in howling more often than other breeds, while the Basenji chortles and yodels but does not bark.

The sounds cats and dogs make are quite different. Cats purr, meow, chirp, chatter, hiss, spit, growl, and scream. Dogs whine, whimper, yelp, growl, bark, and howl. Just what does this cacophony mean? Pets recognize that owners are a verbal species, and tend to aim many vocalizations at humans. For the most part, our pets' vocal repertoire is linked with body language and serves as an indicator of emotion. Vocalizations are used alongside body language the way inflection is used in human speech to impart clearer meaning.

THE SOUND OF CONTENTMENT

Cats are different from dogs in that they seem able to express their pleasure vocally. Some dogs, particularly puppies, will grunt to express contentment, but Kitty trills when she's happy, and purring seems to be an expression of contentment. Louder purrs may be used when the cat is in pain, and some felines even purr as they die. Theories explaining how the purr is produced abound, but currently there is no definitive answer.

Cats purr only when in the company of people or another pet, which indicates that the rumbling sound is intended to be communicative. It's speculated that the purr may be a subtle way of expressing submission.

While the cat's purr is subtle and soothing, the dog's howl is haunting and melancholy. In the wild, howls serve to call the pack together and may be a method of announcing territorial rights. Howls can be a communal activity for dogs, a kind of canine sing-along. One howl—or even a fire engine's siren or human singing—is often enough invitation for every dog within hearing to join the friendly chorus.

But dogs most often howl from loneliness. Nothing is worse for the group-oriented dog than being alone. Dogs howl when separated from their family group; a dog's howl often pleads, "I am here. Come join me."

LOUD DEMANDS

The cat's meows are directed almost exclusively at humans. Cats often develop a repertoire of individual meows, from soft and sweet to loud and drawn out. Meows are a demand for service.

Cats typically meow when they are on the wrong side of a door and want it opened, when they want to be fed, or when they want attention. As Kitty becomes more passionate, the demands turn to complaints, with the sound growing more strident and low-pitched.

POLITE REQUESTS

The equivalent of the demanding feline meow is the canine whine. But dogs tend to beg rather than demand.

Whining is a solicitation to owners which can signify almost anything: play with me, rub my tummy, feed me, notice me. Human children will whine to get their own way, too. Dogs often whine or yelp for attention, but these vocalizations can also signal distress. Whining and whimpering are used to communicate submission, defense, greeting, and pain.

Cats utter requests too, but where meow-demands are aimed at people, chirping and chattering sounds seem to slip out in situations that are beyond Kitty's control. Cats chatter and chirp as a sign of solicitation or of frustration; the unreachable bird outside the window might prompt such a performance.

ALARMING NOISE

Barks are the most commonly used vocal signal in dogs, although barking is rare in wolves. Barks may be used in play or as a greeting, during defense or as a lone call, but they are most often used as a general call for attention, and barking is considered a sign of dominance.

The canine bark is the equivalent of a fire alarm. Dogs usually bark to warn the family group of anything unusual or interesting. This could be the arrival of a stranger or friend, an animal trespassing on the lawn, or even a fly buzzing against the window. Although barking can often sound ferocious, it is not necessarily a sign of aggression. Dogs also bark together for the same reasons they howl together: for the simple joy of making noise. When I pick up my newspaper each morning, the neighbors' dogs begin their barking symphony. It's as if when Duke barks, "There she is!" the others feel compelled to bark back.

Incidentally, yelling at a group of barking dogs rarely makes them stop. They think you're joining in on the happy bark-a-thon or challenging them to a barking contest. Usually the dogs win.

Cats don't have a verbal signal equivalent to the bark. This makes sense, because the cat evolved to hunt and live alone and therefore had no need to warn anybody but himself.

FEARFUL SOUNDS

Both dogs and cats use snarls and growls to get their messages across, and these are often signs of fear. A growl is an intense low-pitched rumble that can be made with the mouth and lips closed. A snarl is the display of teeth, especially the canines, and may or may not be accompanied by sound.

The dog's snarl indicates slight fear, and a growl shows deeper concern; both are warnings to back off. The conflicted dog may bark hysterically and snarl or growl as well, indicating he is probably more frightened than aggressive. Growls are used as a defense, a warning signal. Yelps and yipes emerge when the dog is actually injured or so frightened he can't contain himself.

Cats spit when they are startled, a kind of feline gasp of fright. The feline hiss leaves no room for doubt; it's an audible warning to keep your distance. Snarls and growls, similar to the dog's, indicate an escalation of emotion. Some cats actually scream when terrified or enraged, particularly when engaged in battle with another cat.

FACIAL EXPRESSION

Canine and feline body language are used not only to communicate emotion but also to regulate social distance. The way the pet holds himself, his position in relation to others, and the movement or position of ears, legs, tail, and even fur will serve to invite others to approach or warn them away. Facial expression communicates volumes. By posturing in a certain way, the pet declares himself to be fearful or friendly, aggressive or submissive.

Eyes are very important in pet communication. Eye contact in the form of a direct, unblinking stare is a sign of dominance in both dogs and cats and is considered a challenge; it may even incite some dogs or cats to aggression. Conversely, when the pet averts his eyes, he's showing submission.

You can tell what mood your pets are in by monitoring the position of their eyelids and the dilation of their pupils. The dog's pupils will suddenly dilate wide when he's feeling aggressive or dominant. But just about any strong emotion—fear, pleasure, anger, excitement—can cause Kitty's pupils to suddenly contract to slits. Droopy, sleepy-looking eyelids indicate trust in the cat and pleasure in the dog. Poochie often squints his eyes and moans in ecstasy when his ears are rubbed. Wide-open eyes are the sign of an alert pet. Cats that present their face close to your own with wide-open eyes show trust by leaving their eyes unprotected.

The position of the ears also indicates the pet's mood. When the ears are erect and facing forward, the pet is displaying interest. Forward-facing ears in a dog may also indicate dominance or aggression. And canine ears flatten against the head by degrees depending on how fearful or submissive the dog feels. Similarly, cat ears remain erect but turn to the sides, showing

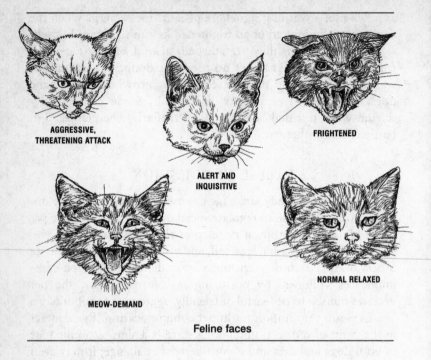

AGGRESSIVE, THREATENING ATTACK

FRIGHTENED

ALERT AND INQUISITIVE

NORMAL RELAXED

MEOW-DEMAND

Feline faces

more of the backs of the ears, when an aggressive Kitty is threatening to attack. Fearful cats flatten their ears tight to the head. Feline readiness to attack is indicated by how much of the back of the ear is visible; the more you can see, the more likely it is that Kitty will strike. And fearfulness can be measured by the degree to which ears are flattened to the cat's head.

The cat's whiskers also tell a story. A relaxed cat's whiskers extend straight out from the muzzle, but when Kitty's interest is aroused, whiskers fan forward until they nearly embrace the object of curiosity. When whiskers are fanned forward and ears are erect but turned sideways, Kitty is signaling aggression and possible attack. When frightened, the cat draws her whiskers backward and slicks them against her cheeks, in the same way she flattens her ears.

Feline grooming can also be an expression of emotion. Called displacement grooming, Kitty often indulges in a sudden bout of furious licking when surprised by something unexpected.

It's theorized that this action is a way for the cat to calm herself down. You may notice this behavior when Kitty accidentally rolls off the sofa or leaps for the windowsill and misses. She'll first glance around to make sure nobody noticed her *faux paw*, then groom herself to clean away the embarrassment.

BODY LANGUAGE

The way your pets carry themselves says a great deal about what they are feeling. In both dogs and cats, an erect posture demonstrates confidence and is the sign of a dominant animal. Dominant dogs may actually seem to rise up on their toes when they want to impress another animal. Confident cats face the unknown head on, their body poised to strike if necessary; so do aggressive dogs who lean forward toward the object of their antipathy.

Cat and dog tails also tell a story. In both dogs and cats, the relaxed pet's tail curves down and back up in a gentle *U* and is typically held higher to show interest. In dogs, a high-held tail is a sign of dominance, confidence, and sometimes aggression, depending on what the rest of the body is doing. But cats greet their superiors (owners or dominant animals) with the tail held straight up with just the end tipped over as though waving hello. Cats will hold their tails straight up with fur bristled like a brush to show aggression. A dog's low-held tail shows submission or fear, while a cat bristles the tail and holds it in an inverted *U* to show fear or defensiveness. And in both species, tucking the tail between the legs is a signal of submission.

But a great deal of canine and feline body language is unique to each species and can seem contradictory tò the uninitiated observer who understands only one of the two languages. The silent semaphore of dog and cat communication becomes even more complex when you realize that something as simple as a wagging tail can have several different meanings, depending on what the rest of the body is doing at the time.

MISUNDERSTANDINGS

Both dogs and cats can make themselves look larger by using *piloerection*, or fluffing up their fur, but the meaning is a bit dif-

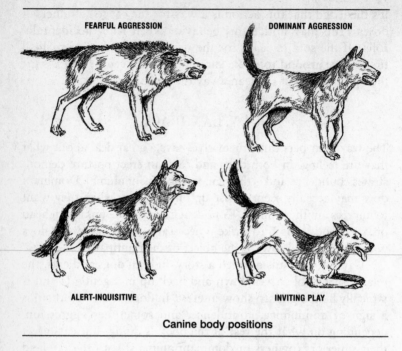

FEARFUL AGGRESSION　　　　　　　**DOMINANT AGGRESSION**

ALERT-INQUISITIVE　　　　　　　**INVITING PLAY**

Canine body positions

ferent for each. When a dog is communicating aggression, the fur will rise in a ridge along the dog's back and shoulders (referred to as the hackles). Cats make the most of this talent by arching their backs and standing sideways to their adversary before they fluff; but rather than signifying aggression, this typical Halloween look is the sign of a frightened cat.

Ironically, when a dog sees a cat self-inflate, he thinks Kitty is being aggressive when actually the cat is scared to death. And the dog with raised hackles may not look like a threat to the cat if she thinks the dog is acting scared.

One of the biggest misunderstandings arises from tail talk. Dogs wag their tails, and so do cats, but the meanings couldn't be more different. In most cases, canine tail wagging is a friendly greeting and is considered a distance-reducing signal that says, "Come here. I want to be your friend." A subordinate dog wags his tail in a loose, wide, low pattern and may even include his

CRYING UNCLE
BUT MAY
STILL ATTACK
IF PRESSED

AGGRESSION WITH
INTENT TO ATTACK

FEARFUL CAT

Feline body positions

hips in the movement. The more dominant dog wags faster in higher, sharper arcs.

The opposite is true of cats, where tail wagging is a distance-increasing signal that says, "Go away. You bother me." When the feline tail lashes or even thumps the floor, it's an unmistakable warning to back off or get smacked.

Obviously, tail wagging is a prime opportunity for interspecies confusion. The dog approaching with a friendly wag is interpreted by the cat to be ready to attack; and the dog seeing the waving feline tail thinks it's an invitation to approach and can't understand why Kitty breaks the rules and slaps his nose.

An aggressive dog may hold his tail tightly arched over his back with just the end jerking very quickly back and forth; this behavior means that attack is imminent, and it is usually accompanied by appropriate facial expression and vocalizations. Cats, too, may flick or twitch the end of the tail as an expression of frustration or irritation, but the tail can be horizontal, vertical, or in any other position with the tip flicking and be more a warning than an announcement of mayhem. When Kitty is ready to attack, instead of holding her tail high like the dog, she will keep it low and close to her body.

Both dogs and cats show submission by trying to look smaller than they are. Cats indicate surrender by flattening themselves on the floor with their ears and tail tucked tight. Dogs also crouch low, plaster their ears to their heads, and tuck in their tails. But a dog will take submission a step further by rolling on his back to bare his unprotected tummy. The ultimate canine sign of submission is urinating in this position or when crouched before the dominant animal.

But rolling on the back doesn't mean the same thing to a cat. Felines, after all, have quite effective claws which can be put to good use from that position. Consider how the cat grapples with a toy mouse, clutching it with her front claws and biting, while the rear claws bunny-kick from beneath. Consequently, when Poochie rolls over, Kitty thinks he's taking a defensive posture like a cat, and reacts accordingly. But when Poochie sees the cat on her back, he thinks she's crying uncle, and gets not one but four sets of claws in the face for his mistake.

Also, the dog who is ready to attack will show his intention in his eyes when his pupils dilate. But when the cat's pupils suddenly dilate to saucer proportions, it indicates fear, not aggression.

One of the first tricks dogs learn is to shake paws. That's because offering the paw is a canine sign of submission and is the prelude to rolling over. Dogs often use this pawing gesture to solicit play or attention. But pawing has just the opposite meaning for cats. Kitty raises a paw as a warning gesture in prelude to unfurling her claws; once again the dog gets an unexpected bop on the nose.

Cats rub against objects to leave their scent behind and use head bumps and rubs or hip leans as they pass by. Face rubbing is thought to be a subtle sign of deference, with the subordinate feline approaching and bumping or rubbing against the dominant pet or person. Nose touches and hip leans are considered by the cat to be gestures of friendship, so feel complimented next time Kitty blesses you.

Dogs also bump and lean, but it's not always friendly and is certainly not submissive. Dogs bump or even push with their chests and lean with their bodies against people or other animals as a sign of dominance. So when Kitty rubs or leans against the dog, Poochie thinks the cat is showing dominance, when actually Kitty is signifying just the opposite. Cats show dominance by pointedly scratching objects in the presence of another cat or a dog they want to impress.

INTERPRETING PET SIGNALS

Cat and dog gestures and vocalizations vary somewhat from pet to pet, just as people have different accents, dialects, or colloquial ways of saying things. And pets may signal ambivalent feelings by showing aspects of both dominance and submission when they aren't sure how to react in a given situation. The dog's front half may snarl while the tail wags a welcome, or the cat's tail may thrash while he purrs. You won't understand what your dog or cat is saying simply by watching the ears or the tail; to get the whole picture, you must place pet communication in context alongside vocalizations and whole-body signals.

It's impossible to describe every possible combination of signals, but a few examples of whole-body communications will offer you some perspective. Overall, cats and dogs communicate to increase or decrease the distance between them and another. This protects the pet's personal space from invasion. How the pet feels about the other person or animal determines whether he will invite closer proximity or try to repel it.

Aggressive Signals

Dogs and cats begin their aggressive acts with threats to warn off interlopers. Depending on the response from the other party, threats increase by degree until they reach attack.

Dogs threaten with a direct stare accompanied by a low growl. The threatening snarl pushes the lips forward and up to reveal the canine (long) teeth. The ears are pointed forward, the hackles rise, and the dog arches his neck, holds his head high, and leans forward. He walks stiffly and may raise one leg to urinate and then claw the ground. As aggression escalates, the growls get louder, the tail is held higher, either in a stationary position or with only a stiff, rapid wag of aggression. When attack becomes imminent, the dog's pupils dilate, and he may lower his head and extend his neck as though "pointing" his adversary, while he twists his ears out and down or plasters them to the sides of his head, perhaps to protect them.

The cat also threatens with a direct stare. She faces her adversary head on, points her ears forward, and holds her head high with her neck arched. Her tail curves in a scimitar shape down and horizontally away from her body as a sign of assertiveness. The other animal must avert its eyes to say, "I want no trouble." But if eye contact is returned, the threatening cat's ears stay erect but turn to the sides, and she circles the other animal trying to make it back down. She may hiss and fluff her fur to appear larger, until she proceeds to the more serious growls. A pair of cats may posture for more than fifteen minutes trying to get each other to back down. Attack is rarely necessary; the cat who gives up and runs away is the loser. But sometimes neither will give an inch. The pupils of the cat's eyes contract to slits, her tail comes close to her body, and she lowers her head and stretches her neck forward, horizontal with her body, when ready to attack.

Fearful Signs

Cats that are frightened show many of the same signs of the aggressive cat, but they tend to be more vocal. The startled cat may spit in addition to hissing. Instead of facing the threat head on, the scared feline turns sideways, arches her back, and fluffs out her fur, trying to bluff her way out of the situation by looking as big and threatening as possible. She folds her ears down and sideways like little airplane wings, and her pupils dilate. When she realizes the bluff won't work, she compresses herself to look as small as possible; she crouches, pulls her paws and tail close to her body, and draws her head in, all the while hissing and growling ferociously. The cat will either be forced to defend herself or will turn tail and run, conceding defeat.

Dogs that are fearful also make themselves look small. When confronted by a dominant or aggressive individual, the fearful dog's hackles rise. He averts his eyes, lays his ears down, and leans backward. He may snarl, growl, and bark, but he will pull his lips back rather than pushing them forward and up, revealing more teeth in a submissive grin. He tucks his tail tightly between his legs, and he may wag it in this low position. To signal submission, he crouches, rolls onto his back to present his belly, and urinates in the ultimate display.

Be aware that dogs and cats who exhibit fear are just as likely—probably *more* likely—to injure another pet or the owner when they attempt to defend themselves.

Friendly Gestures

Dogs and cats use some of the signals of antagonism as invitations to play—stalking and pouncing, chasing and pawing. The pet signals it's just pretend or play fighting by leaving out the emotional language of vocalizations or by using exaggerated body movements that contradict the negative signals. Dogs wag their whole body, and cats keep their claws in.

The most obvious play signal is the *lordosis position,* which is also used by females to invite mating, and called the play bow when used by dogs. In this position the pet's front end is down while the rear end is up. A dog will wag his tail in a happy invitation or offer his forepaws one after another. Sometimes the dog will bow and then leap forward to poke with his nose or bow and then leap away as invitation to a game of chase.

Cats may tiptoe about sideways or pat an object or another pet and then leap away to suggest a game of tag. Sometimes the cat will roll about on the floor, keeping her ears erect and her claws contained, to prompt play or petting.

Cats often greet their owners with a special meow and run toward them with their tail held high with just the end tipped over. An elaborate ritual of rubbing against the person's ankles may then ensue. Dogs also greet owners by bounding forward and perhaps dancing around, barking, and tail-wagging. A dog may acknowledge your dominance by crouching and wagging his tail in a low position, rolling over, or even urinating.

A dog may use certain signals that most people interpret as apologetic, though they actually represent the ultimate form of submission—pressing his ears flat, pulling his lips back horizontally in a submissive grin, crouching, crawling on his belly while lifting a paw, and wagging his tail in the lowest possible position. Flicking the tongue out is a signal of intent to lick. Licking your face or hands is an appeasement gesture, and dogs that are reprimanded often aim their attention there. Submissive urination is absolute deference in dog language. A dog often uses this repertoire with an owner or another dog or pet that is dominant; these signals are intended to decrease the distance between them.

Cats may purr to signal good intentions. They present their faces and rub their cheeks and chins against dominant people or other pets as a sign of affection, a sharing of the scent between friendly acquaintances. They also communicate affection and trust by sharing close proximity with others. Sleeping or eating together, mutual grooming, and engaging in play are the cat's declarations of devotion. Sleeping in another's presence, especially with his back to the other, is the ultimate sign of trust.

Dogs and cats have a number of gestures in common that mean different things to each and that can cause misunderstandings. But when raised together, dogs and cats easily learn each other's language and get along well. Even pets that have never before experienced a "foreign" species can and do learn, and they rarely suffer more than fleeting discomfort during the schooling process.

In fact, cats and dogs learn each other's language more quickly if allowed to experience some of the consequences. A swat on the nose from a cat or the cat being rolled onto her back by the dog won't hurt anything but feelings.

That's not to say you should allow a pet to be seriously injured. Posturing is fine, but signs of overt aggression—imminent attack—should be interrupted; you should not allow your pets to actually engage in a fight.

Always remove the subordinate animal from the situation so that the dominant pet won't get his nose out of joint and feel a need to escalate the lesson. But when you're separating dueling pets, take care to avoid getting scratched or bitten yourself.

A long-distance squirt of water from a plant sprayer is often enough to distract the antagonists. If they are actually fighting, try dumping a glass of water on them or tossing a pillow or a blanket over the pair to give them something else to think about while you're getting the upper hand. See Chapter 15 for more tips on introducing pets to each other and smoothing relationships.

In addition to learning each other's language, pets must be able to understand humans as well. Cats and dogs are so attuned to body signals that they can often "read" intentions we don't realize we're broadcasting. That's why Poochie always knows ahead of time that you're planning to give him a bath, and it's the reason cats hide when a veterinary trip is in the works.

If we know what to watch for, pets make their intentions very clear in an effort to tell their dense human owners what they want. However, pets also need to understand what owners want them to do. And owners need to learn how to enforce the rules of the house.

CHAPTER FOURTEEN

Cats Lead, Dogs Follow

Popular theory says dogs are easy to teach while cats are untrainable. The truth is, both are intelligent and eager to learn. They would have died out aeons ago if that had not been the case.

The difficulty is not with pets but with the perception of what training should be. The trainability of your cats and dogs hinges not only on their intelligence and ability to learn but also on your willingness to teach.

You must be confident that your pets can be trained. Trust me on this one—they can. In fact, you've been training your dogs and cats since the first moment they entered your life.

THE PROPER ATTITUDE

To teach your pets anything, you must also understand what they "hear" you telling them—it's not always what you intend. Just as misunderstandings occur when dog language is read by cats and vice versa, people commonly confuse their pets by sending contradictory signals.

Dogs and cats understand much more than owners give them credit for. But, what we tell them silently with posture and gesture carries much more weight than words.

If you verbally chastise your pet but smile at the same time, the pet knows you aren't serious. Similarly, your tone of voice and the emotion it conveys are more significant than your actual words. During training, recognize and pay attention to what you are telling your pet, both verbally and silently, because the pet will.

To be a teacher, you must be the dominant member of your family group. This does not mean that you have to fight with your pets, just subtly remind them that you are in charge. Do this by speaking the language of the dog and cat.

In both species, the dominant individual moves and vocalizes with confidence, stands tall, and makes eye contact. So should you. When you want your pets to do something, use a calm, confident tone of voice, remembering that emotion gets the message across more than words. An angry or strident tone isn't confident; it's aggressive. A loud, shrill voice teaches pets either to avoid you or to become defensive at the perceived threat.

Remember also that dominant dogs and cats practice chivalry, and so should you. Once dominance has been acknowledged and the subordinate has cried uncle, let him off the hook and don't rub it in. Make eye contact with your pet only until he looks away; continuing to stare after this sign of deference is confusing—the pet has done his part, after all. In some animals, extended staring may lead to defensive actions.

Finally, understand that you don't have to be "above" your pet twenty-four hours a day. Leaders can relax the rules and still retain their status; dogs and cats do it all the time. Lead Dog "pretends" to be submissive by play-bowing to a subordinate in order to instigate a game. And King Cat enjoys the ministrations of other cats, sleeping with them or grooming them. After the games or social interaction, the dominant animal always subtly reminds the others of his status. And so should you.

Establishing your position in the household will not distance you from your pets; it will bring you closer to them. Submissive pets in a social group typically compete with one another for the attention of, and interaction with, the leader. You'll be smothered in furry love.

THE INTELLIGENCE OF DOGS, CATS, AND PEOPLE

Pet intelligence is related more to form and function than to any other measure. Scent-oriented dogs might find a hidden ball, while vision-oriented cats might not. Paw-oriented cats and doggy diggers might be better equipped to claw objects from beneath a shielding cover, while that thought might never cross the mind of a racer like the Afghan Hound. Dogs and cats, in other words, are as smart as they need to be.

It is most important for you to be smarter than your pet. Like observant children, the smart pet knows all the right buttons to push to get people to do what he wants. Face it, you've been trained by the best.

HOW PETS LEARN

Pets learn the same way people do. *Classical conditioning* begins at the moment of birth and results when the pet forms an association between an external event (like a trip to the vet) and an involuntary reaction (shots or, better yet, a treat). Depending on the reaction, the pet then associates the event with something pleasant or unpleasant and reacts accordingly.

Learning occurs through trial and error. The puppy learns to root beneath a blanket to find the hidden toy, and success is the reward. And a great deal of learning occurs from direct instruction. The subordinate pet is *told* what to do by the dominant one when Lead Dog rolls Puppy onto his back to enforce a submissive posture, and when King Cat disciplines Kitten, who has the temerity to play with his tail.

Classical conditioning is useful in training, but it can backfire unless it's timed correctly. Pets have a very limited sense of time, and the involuntary reaction must occur simultaneously with, or *immediately* following, the external event for the association to be made. For instance, a pet that's swatted with a newspaper too long after the misdeed will not associate the swat with peeing on the carpet; instead, the pet associates the newspaper with fear, and may later attack the newspaper or anyone carrying one.

Some learning takes place by passive example, as when the mother cat shows kittens what to do in the litter box or when the dog learns to fear cats by watching another dog's reaction. Cats and dogs also learn by watching their owners. If you react with excitement and rush to answer the doorbell, you can bet your pets will learn to react similarly.

Pets learn our language through trial and error and sometimes by passive example, if another pet is present who is more familiar with the lingo. But despite evidence to the contrary, dogs and cats are not mind readers and must learn the rules of the house through direct instruction.

The elements of training are simple and are based on conditioned response. Called *operant conditioning*, this training method is based on the fact that an action by the pet can result in either positive (pleasant) or negative (unpleasant) reinforcement. For instance, the dog barks at the mailman (action), and the mailman leaves the yard (positive reinforcement). The dog has taught himself that barking will make an undesirable person leave.

Your pet uses the same method to train you. The pet wants to be fed, so he creates a stimulus (barks, meows, whatever). When that stimulus causes the desired response (you feed him), he stops agitating. The cessation of the obnoxious barking or meowing rewards you for feeding him and reinforces your response; the next time the pet barks or meows, you'll put down food. And by feeding him on demand, you have reinforced your pet's barking or meowing behavior; the next time he wants food, he knows what to do.

Training cats and dogs is done in the same way. The trainer elicits the desired *response* by applying the proper *stimulus* and then positively *reinforcing* (rewarding) the desired behavior when the proper response is made.

Negative reinforcement, on the other hand, is something usually to be avoided. So-called choke, prong, or electric-shock collars have historically been used in training dogs. Despite their names, they are designed to distract and not to hurt the dog, and can be humane training tools when used by knowledgeable and ethical professionals. However, they can very easily be misused, and are dangerous in the wrong hands. Improper use can physically injure or emotionally scar your dog, prompting behavior problems that are hard to resolve. Avoid these collars. Dogs are extremely forgiving and put up with a lot of unpleasantness, but pain is counterproductive to training and to a positive pet relationship. Cats are even less forgiving. A painful experience will prompt Kitty to look for a new owner.

Negative reinforcement (I prefer to call it correction) is effective only when timed appropriately, and it should never be painful. Pain has no place in building a loving pet-owner relationship, and it will compromise the bond between you and your cat or dog. Positive reinforcement is more effective, and it will strengthen your relationship with the pet.

Operant conditioning is an effective method of training both dogs and cats. But both the stimulus and the reinforcement elements of training are very different for each.

INSPIRATION AND PERSPIRATION

Dogs aim to please you, while cats please themselves. This is only natural, considering the social structures they come from, so it is basic to the way each must be trained. In order to train your pets, you must discover what inspires them to action and what correction is most effective.

For most dogs, sufficient inspiration consists of praise from their owner. A simple "good dog" is all that's needed to keep most dogs on the straight and narrow. That's because dogs have been bred to *want* to do what they're told, and they struggle mightily to please us. But dogs are individuals, and what works for one may not work for another. Poochie's most favorite thing in life—perhaps his ball, an old sock toy, or a special treat—may be the perfect incentive.

For an effective form of correction, figure out what Poochie considers the absolutely worst thing that could happen to him. Usually, it's being ignored, being left alone, or disappointing the leader. Dogs are so social that disapproval or being shunned by their leader is considered worse than death. Verbal shaming as well as a time-out in a room by himself are two very effective corrections. They sting for only the first few minutes, however, so don't prolong the agony any longer than that. By using mostly positive reinforcements along with a few judicial negative ones, you can train your dog quite easily. Ultimately, the hardest part is getting Poochie to understand what you want.

Cats, on the other paw, have a "what's in it for me?" attitude. Sure, they love you and all that, but it is contrary to the feline nature to do another's bidding. Requests need to make sense for the cat to want to do them. Just as dog training builds on the canine's inherent tendency to follow the leader, cat training must be based on the cat's natural inclination to do things her own way. The key to cat training is discovering what the cat wants and using that to get her to do what you want. You can't *make* a cat do anything, but you can *entice* her to want to do something.

What inspires cats? Different things, depending on the circumstances, but the two most universal feline motivators are predatory opportunity and food. You can train some cats to do back flips for the right treat or toy. If Kitty has a favorite toy, reserve it as a reward for work well done, and don't allow her to play with that toy at any other time. Treats work best if they are different from the cat's regular diet. Try a favorite strongly scented flavor of Kitty's regular canned diet, and reserve bribes only for training. Canned treats will work much better with a cat who is fed a dry diet.

Ignoring or even shaming a cat rarely has as much impact as it does for dogs. While Poochie fears being left alone, cats hate the unexpected. A well-placed squirt of water that soaks her tail, or an unexpected noise—like a "Ssssttt!" cat-hiss from you— can be particularly effective in dissuading Kitty from indulging in unwanted behavior.

It will take both inspiration and perspiration—yours and theirs—to train your pets properly.

CONSISTENT PATIENCE

One of the most important and misunderstood components of pet training is consistency. Cats and dogs will not get the message clearly if the rules keep changing. Besides, inconsistency is not fair to you or the pet and will only cause more problems down the road.

A classic example is teaching the pet to "come." You confuse the dickens out of a pet when he's given the "come" command, obeys, and then is corrected for some misdeed. The poor pet associates obeying with the correction, so what does he do next time? He doesn't know if he'll be rewarded or corrected for obeying.

Dogs and cats cannot differentiate between what's appropriate and what's incorrect unless they are given consistently enforced guidelines. If you don't want the pet on the sofa, there should be no exceptions—ever. Allowing him on the sofa one day, then correcting him the next only confuses the pet. Unless consistency is enforced, the pet won't even try to follow the rules, because whatever he does may be okay or wrong according to your mood.

The human members of your family must agree to the rules. It's not going to promote good training if the dog or cat knows that one human member is a softie. The pet will act just like a kid who goes to one parent to solicit a favor after the other parent has refused the request.

Decide what key words or signals you will use. It's easiest to use the same ones for both the dog and cat. Your message must be made as simple and easy to understand as possible. Single-syllable one-word commands, like "come" and "no," are by far the most effective. Choose one command for one action and stick to it. You know that "no," "stop it," and "quit it" mean the same thing, as do "come," "here, boy," and "come here." But all these variations are confusing for the pet. Also decide on a release command, a signal that tells your pets they can go about their business. "Okay" is a good one.

Pets also respond well to clear-cut hand signals and to sounds like whistles or clickers. The pet learns to associate the signal or command with the appropriate action and/or reward. In other words, when you say "sit," the pet performs the action and sits. You could as easily say "bird" and the pet would sit, if that's the meaning he's been taught.

Finally, remember always to link a command for action and any positive reinforcement, or reward, with your pet's name. Say, "Kitty, come" or "Good boy, Poochie!"

But when using negative reinforcement or a cease-and-desist command, do not use the pet's name. Say, "No, shame on you!" or "Sssssssttt!" along with a water squirt. Your cat and dog should associate their names only with good, positive things that come from you.

Patience is the key to success. Think of your pets as having the attention span of children, and you're on the right track. Teach only one thing at a time, in ten- to fifteen-minute training sessions perhaps three or four times a day. Short and frequent lessons are more effective than a single marathon training session. Train *before* the pet eats, not after; a full tummy prompts a nap, not concentration. And don't move on to teaching the next command until you're convinced the pet understands the first, whether he performs consistently or not.

Your goal in training is to make the experience fun for you and for the pet. If you turn training into a game, your pets will become willing accomplices in their own education.

THAT'S ME

The most important word your pet can learn is his own name. Use his name whenever possible, especially when greeting him and when you praise his behavior.

Talk to your pets, and they will learn to listen to you. It's not important that they understand every word. What's important is that they pay attention when you speak to them. Their name spoken by you is their cue to concentrate on what you're saying, so they won't miss out on instruction, praise, or a treat. That's critical in training.

Be careful to make distinctions between your pets so that they will learn not only their own name but the names of the other pets as well. You want Poochie to know you're talking to him and not to Kitty.

Identify your pet's property by using the pet's name in conjunction with the item. It's not just a toy, it's "Kitty's mouse" or "Poochie's ball." By using your pets' names, you'll help give them a sense of self that they need in order to enjoy a special relationship with you and with each other.

"NO!"

Probably the second most important word your pets can learn is "no." The command is used to interrupt and halt any objectionable behavior, from digging in the flower bed to chewing shoes or scratching the furniture. It can even save your pet's life when you prevent him from eating something dangerous or from crossing the road.

Your tone must be commanding yet somehow different from your everyday voice. Use the same manner you would use with a recalcitrant child—no-nonsense and matter-of-fact. Remember that the cat's meow and the dog's growl drop in pitch the more demanding they become, and rise in pitch when they are uncertain or fearful; keep your voice deep and authoritative. Pets will recognize the no-nonsense tone and will soon understand the word's meaning.

The sudden forceful sound of your voice on this single syllable is more effective than shouting and is often adequate to interrupt bad behavior. But until your pet learns the meaning of the word, you'll need to interrupt the action in some other way.

There are a number of effective methods of interrupting poor pet behavior. A squirt gun or plant mister aimed at the tail will work particularly well with cats. Another method is to shake a noisemaker like a coffee can filled with marbles or pennies. Tossing a soft object like a pillow or bean bag toward the pet—*without* making contact—is another concentration-breaker. Time your "no!" to coincide with the interrupting object. Eventually Poochie and Kitty will learn to stop what they're doing when they hear the word, and the physical reminder will no longer be needed.

Interrupting the behavior is not enough to teach the lesson, however. After the stimulus produces the desired effect, you must use positive reinforcement to hammer the lesson home. As soon as the "no" stops the objectionable behavior, give the pet a reward.

Always use verbal praise—"Good Kitty" or "Good Poochie"—to acknowledge the pet's proper response. You want your pet to know that he's done something right. It doesn't matter at first whether or not the pet understands *what* he's done right; that will come later with repetition. Along with the verbal praise, also reinforce the behavior with your pet's favorite reward, like a treat.

Please take care not to overuse "no." Some pets hear this word so often that they think it's their name. When cats and dogs get little quality attention from their owners, they may act up just to get noticed. After all, even a "No! Bad dog!" is better than being ignored.

One final note. Train your pets one at a time, as they can be easily distracted. In the beginning, keep things simple; concentrate on one pet at a time and one lesson at a time.

LEASH TRAINING

Leash training is extremely important for your pet. A leash offers much-needed control and enforces commands when the voice isn't enough. In fact, in some parts of the country, laws prohibit owners from allowing unleashed dogs to leave their property.

Accepting a leash is the pet's ticket to freedom. The dog and cat that are leash-trained are allowed to accompany owners to more places. It's also much easier to teach other commands, and even to bathe the pet, when he is under leash control.

Both dogs and cats should wear collars with appropriate identification at all times. However, the cat's neck is structurally more delicate than the dog's, and a safety "breakaway" collar is most appropriate for Kitty. In the event that Kitty catches the collar on something, the collar gives rather than the cat's neck.

The leash may be attached to the dog's collar or to a harness, while a figure-eight harness is the tool of choice for cats. The first step is simply to place the collar or harness on the pet and let him get used to the idea. Some pets don't seem to notice, and go about their normal routine, while others complain, roll about, refuse to move, or throw a fit.

If your pet is a complainer, shower him with lots of positive reinforcement while he's wearing the new gear. Give him a treat, or play a game to distract him, all the while telling Kitty or Poochie what a wonderfully intelligent creature he is. Let him wear the gear for ten minutes or so, and then give him a break. Repeat the lesson in ten-minute sessions three or four times a day for a week.

Once the pet accepts the collar or harness, clip on the leash. Let the cat or dog drag the leash about, making sure it doesn't get tangled up in the furniture. Again, expose each pet to the leash in five- to ten-minute sessions three or four times a day for a week or so, until he's well used to the idea. Next, simply pick up your end of the leash. Follow the pet around, letting him do the leading for now. Try to keep slack in the leash, and don't allow the cat or dog to tug you around. The idea is for you eventually to lead your pet, not the other way around, and if you let him get away with tugging now, you'll only have to untrain him later.

Finally, use your pet's favorite reward to inspire him to follow the leash direction. Gently tug on the leash, then *immediately* release it, calling the pet's name as you do so. Flaunt the toy or treat until the dog or cat comes to you, and give him the reward with lots of verbal praise.

Dragging your pet with the leash will not work. Big dogs will simply sit or lie down, and cats will look at you as if you've lost your mind. Head halters are available for dogs, which fit like the facial gear used on horses. These can be effective with larger, more stubborn dogs; basically, where his face points, he will follow.

For both cats and dogs, the biggest hurdle usually is getting the pet to understand the notion of following you on the leash. Use a treat or a feather toy, a ball or vocal praise, or whatever works, to keep your dog or cat at your side as you begin to walk. Give short tug-release instructions, followed by praise and an occasional toy or treat reinforcement to keep the pet walking with you.

Once Kitty and Poochie are walking comfortably on the leash while inside the house, try outdoor excursions. Don't forget your equipment, incentives and all. Eventually you'll be able to go for walks with your pets, secure in the freedom of the leash, and the walk itself will be incentive enough for all.

"COME"

The easiest way to train your pet to come to you consistently is to use the feeding opportunity to your advantage. Both cats and dogs come in answer to the whir of the can opener or the clatter of kibble hitting the bowl. Use that sound to train your pets to come when called.

The idea is to replace the trigger sound with the command "Come." Do this by using the command, linked with the pet's name, at the same time as the trigger he's already responding to. As the kibble hits the bowl, call, "Poochie, come!" and then praise and feed him when he does.

Stay alert for such opportunities. If the cat or dog always greets you upon your return home, have a special treat or toy ready. As you see the pet approaching, give the command "Kitty, come!" (don't forget to use the pet's name), and then reward her when she does.

A great way to train dogs to come is to capitalize on their love of the chase. During a game, turn and run away from the dog, inviting him to come along with your command. When he does, stop and reward him with appropriate praise.

Use a toy to lure your cat; fishing pole–style toys are excellent for this purpose. Drag the toy along the floor toward you, and as the cat approaches, give the "Come" command. Allow Kitty to catch the lure only when she does come to you, and praise her so she knows she's the smartest cat in all catdom.

If you're using treats, be sure to secrete them in your hands or pockets well ahead of time. Don't let the pet see you take out the treat, or you'll train her to come only when you rattle the box or open the refrigerator. Always reward your pets for coming to you on command so they associate their name and the behavior with good things, like positive attention, play, or treats.

Once they've learned the lesson, use rewards randomly to reinforce the training. Ideally, your pets will come when they're called whether you give them a treat or not, because they never know when something good might happen.

Never call your pet to come, and then punish or chastise him. By doing this, you will undermine all your training. Don't call him to come if you need to correct the pet, trim his toenails, bathe him, or do something that he considers equally distasteful. Go and get him instead.

"SIT"

You can train your pets to sit by using some of the same techniques you used to teach the "Come" command. Watch for an opportunity—when the Kitty or Poochie tail is just about to con-

tact the linoleum, for instance. Then give the command, and
reward the action. Remember to use the pet's name, as in
"Poochie, sit," or "Kitty, sit."

Another technique that works well is to use the stimulus
object—a squeaky ball or a food tidbit—to guide your pet into the
proper position. Hold the attention-grabbing object directly over
your pet's head. When he looks up, move the object slightly
toward him, so he has to continue to raise his head to follow the
object with his eyes. With a bit of luck, Poochie or Kitty will need
to sit to keep from losing her balance. As her tail begins its descent,
give the command, "Poochie, sit," or "Kitty, sit." When she does
so, reward her with verbal praise and let her take the object.

Gentle positioning works better with dogs than with cats. To
use this technique, simply place one hand beneath your dog's
chin and raise it up while gently pressing down on his hips to
induce a sit, and give the command at the same time. Reward the
pet as soon as he assumes the correct position. For some pets it
works better to gently press behind the rear legs instead of on
the hips. It's the same as if someone pushed you behind the
knees: you must sit.

Hint: With very small dogs, and especially with cats, working on a table is helpful. When pets are at floor level, you'll need
to lower yourself to train, and that's not a good body position
for the leader to take, as it undermines your authority.

Continue to practice the "sit" command until the pet is
pretty consistent. Remember to work in an area with few distractions, and only for ten to fifteen minutes at a time. An ideal
time to practice the sit is at your pet's mealtime. Have the cat or
dog sit, then reward him with the full bowl.

"DOWN"

For the "down" command, place the pet in the sit position first.
For a dog, pat the floor in front of him, and give the command
"Down, Poochie." You may need to gently move the dog's front
legs forward. Roll him on his side if necessary, then praise him
while you rub his tummy. Continue practicing until he'll lie
down on just the voice command or the floor-patting signal.

Training cats to obey the "down" command is best done on a tabletop. Place Kitty in a sit and then hold the toy or treat in front of her face and lower it slowly to below table level. The cat's face should follow the reward downward, and the body will follow until she's lying down. Reward Kitty with lots of praise and the treat.

"OFF"

The "off" command is particularly appropriate for cats who tend to climb on top of anything that doesn't move. Some perches, like the top of the television set or the newel post, may be appropriate. Others, like the dining room table, you may consider forbidden.

The technique for reinforcing the "off" command resembles that for the "no" command. Use a spray of water or some other negative incentive to remove Kitty's furry behind. When this is done correctly, the cat should not associate the water with you but should perceive it only as a bolt from cat heaven. As the water hits her tail, say, "Off!" When she does disembark, praise and reward her. You should be able to teach Kitty which perches are available to her and which are your own personal property and not meant for her lounging.

Be aware, however, that a dominant-type cat will probably bow to your power only when you are present. She'll figure it's a time-share situation, and when you're away she'll take temporary possession of the territory.

Your pet can learn to do many other things with just a little encouragement from you. Watch for the things your pets enjoy doing naturally. All you need to do then is give the behavior a name, and teach that name to the pet so that it becomes a command.

Does Poochie like to bring you toys? Teach him the command "fetch." When Kitty plays, does she paw at objects? Teach her to "wave" hello. If Poochie dances on his hind legs, there's a "beg" in there somewhere. And the cat that's a leaper should learn to jump to your shoulder or into your arms on command with little persuasion.

Remember always to end a training session on a pleasant note, so the pet will look forward to your next session. Is the current lesson not going well? Return to a command the pet knows and let him finish the session with success. End with a game you both enjoy.

It is very important to limit the rewards to those instances when your pet actually earns them. The member of the social group who controls access to food, attention, and toys automatically becomes the highest-ranking individual. So when you'd like to interact with your pets, or when they approach you and you're of a mind to accept their attention, first have them earn it. The next time Poochie brings you his ball for a game, or the cat sidles up to your leg and begs for a session of lap-cuddling, place the pet in a "sit" or "down" and then offer the reward by playing fetch or stroking. Your pets have earned it, and you've reinforced your role in their lives.

The key to training the dog and cat in your home is to give them unmistakable boundaries and rules by which to live. They will be happier when they know what's expected of them and what their place in the scheme of things is.

Although some problems may be inevitable when living with dogs and cats together, nothing is insurmountable. The best way to deal with conflicts is to reduce the opportunities for mistakes, both yours and theirs.

CHAPTER FIFTEEN

When Worlds Collide

In the best of all possible worlds, the puppy and kitten grow up together and accept each other as part of one big happy family. Bringing these species together during their prime socialization period best prepares them for living together in peace and harmony as adults. In the real world, however, that rarely happens. But with careful introductions, you can smooth out the bumps along the way or even eliminate them altogether.

It's helpful to understand what your dog and cat expect during introductions. Cats are so attuned to their environment that place exploration takes precedence over investigation of a strange animal. Kitty will be amenable to meeting the dog only when she's comfortable with her surroundings. Then lots of circling will take place, with both pets doing their best to sniff each other without themselves being sniffed.

Although every situation is different and there are always exceptions, it is helpful to keep in mind a few general rules.

THE TEN COMMANDMENTS OF PET DYNAMICS

1. Introductions are much simpler when your resident pet already knows the rules of the house and is familiar with basic obedience commands. Review Chapter 14; at a minimum the resident Poochie or Kitty should understand "no," and Poochie should be leash-trained.

2. It's easier to introduce a newcomer cat to a resident dog than the other way around. The more socially oriented dog tends

to be more accepting of newcomers than a cat would be. Dogs also become easily bored and enjoy change, and a new playmate often is just the ticket. Cats prefer the status quo, however, and may perceive any kind of change as a threat.

3. Resident adult pets tend to accept youngsters more readily than a newcomer adult. A baby is less likely to challenge the resident pet's social status.

4. The more available space you have, the less trouble you will face. Dogs and cats are both territorial creatures. When there's enough room to go around, there's less reason for them to squabble. Living on top of each other increases the likelihood that pets will quarrel over territory. A good rule of thumb is, have no more pets than there are rooms available in your home. When space is at a premium, you must enrich the environment appropriately by offering more hiding places, toys, and lookout posts to keep your pets occupied. Privacy is important to pets. All dogs and cats need a place they can call their own, an inviolable sanctuary where they can retreat from the world and not be bothered by the other pets.

5. Both pets should be familiar with the territory before introductions are made. Often suggestions are made that stranger pets be introduced on neutral ground. With two dogs you can take them to the park, but this isn't practical with cat-dog introductions, which must take place in the house. To even the playing field, you should allow the new pet to explore your home prior to introductions without interference from the resident pet.

6. Choosing complementary pet personalities promotes good relationships. The potential for the most problems occurs when two aggressive individuals are thrown together, especially when there is a great size difference. Confidence is an asset; fear can be problematic. You'll have less trouble if your resident pet is outgoing, curious, and interested, racing to investigate rather than running to hide.

7. Matching a lap-sitter with a playful pet works well, because they don't challenge each other's preferred state of being.

The playful pet may encourage a lap-potato pet to become more active, and the more sedentary pet may help calm down the energetic, on-the-go pet.

8. Introduce a new pet to one resident pet at a time. It's not fair to the newcomer to be faced with a contingent of old-timers, and it's difficult for you to supervise more than two at a time.

9. Pay more attention to the resident pet. Yes, it's hard to dismiss that cute new kitten or puppy, but your resident pet will feel much more willing to accept the newcomer if she doesn't feel that the newcomer has usurped your affections.

10. Finally, patience is the key to successful com*pet*ability. That sounds simplistic, but it's true. Don't expect pets to become fast friends after one nose-to-nose sniff; it can be hate at first sight, and the best one can hope for in these instances is tolerance. More likely, it will take days to weeks before the pets figure out everybody's place and establish their own furry rules.

PET INTRODUCTIONS 101

These basic principles apply no matter what age or species of pet you're introducing to the resident pet. Before anything else, you must consider the resident pet's feelings. He's always had you and the house to himself, and now he must share. Often his first reaction to an interloper is "Nobody asked *me* if I wanted a friend!"

Introduce the new pet in stages whenever possible. Rub or pet the newcomer with a small towel or sock, then bring home the scented item and leave it on the floor where your resident pet will find it. Don't point it out to him and make a big deal out of it. Let the resident pet thoroughly investigate the new smell at his leisure. You should also tape-record the sound of the new pet meowing or barking and play it for the resident pet. Your goal is to make the newcomer somewhat familiar before introductions. Start introducing the sounds and smells a couple of weeks before the actual meeting.

If the resident pet is a cat, have a friend bring in the new pet—that will give your cat less to blame on you. But when the resident is a dog, you should bring in the newcomer yourself to make a statement, because the dog will be looking to you for guidance. You should prepare a room where you can segregate the newcomer from the resident during initial introductions. That way, only a portion of the resident pet's territory will have been violated.

Cats in particular dislike change, so ease the resident cat into the new routine gradually. A dog or puppy will require time for walks, feeding, and grooming; insert these into your schedule *before* the new dog arrives. If parts of the house will be off-limits, make the changes early on. If food bowls or litter boxes need to be relocated, plan ahead. Kitty will have enough to worry about just getting used to the new pet. Accustom her to other disruptions beforehand.

DOG MEETS NEW FELINE

If your dog is the excitable type, place him on a leash before you bring in the new kitten or cat. The newcomer should be in a carrier, giving both pets protection and security, while also providing them the opportunity to see and perhaps to sniff each other through the grille.

After a few minutes take the dog outside for a romp while a friend supervises the feline's exploration of the house. You want Kitty to be familiar with the territory so that there are no distractions during the eventual introductions.

Before you bring the dog back indoors, segregate the cat in the chosen room, where all the comforts of home should already be in place—scratching post, litter box, food and water bowls. Set the carrier on the floor, and let the newcomer out to explore her private chamber by herself.

Once the door to the cat's room is securely closed, let Poochie back into the house. He'll be happy to sniff all the places Kitty has been, which will help further familiarize him with the newcomer. The pair may even exchange sniffs or paw-pats beneath the door. This is a very favorable sign. Separate the two for at least a day before proceeding, and for a longer period if there are any signs of antagonism, such as hisses from Kitty or growls from the dog.

The next step is the nose-to-nose meeting. Feeding both pets ahead of time seems to calm frazzled nerves. Place Poochie on a leash, and open the door to the cat's room. Do not force the encounter; allow the cat to come to the dog. Speak calmly to Poochie in a low voice. If you act excited, he'll get excited and could inadvertently hurt the newcomer. Watch the dog's body language and listen to his vocalizations for cues to his emotional state. Interested and happy is fine; aggressive or predatory is not.

Help your dog control any actions that the cat or kitten might not understand. He may try to place his paw across Kitty's back as a sign of dominance without realizing his own strength. Adult cats can often hold their own with small- to medium-size dogs and even with large dogs that can be dominated, but kittens are at a disadvantage and need a bit of protection. If the dog bothers Kitty too much, have Poochie practice "sit" and allow the two together only when Poochie can control himself. Keeping your dog under leash control helps you avert Poochie being scratched. However, a swat from Kitty won't hurt the dog and can best teach him to respect the cat's space.

Supervise all cat-dog interactions until you are confident that Poochie understands the newcomer is a part of his family and is not to be hurt. Never leave a kitten alone with an adult dog, no matter how well you think they like each other. Accidents happen, and it takes only one mistake to cause serious injury.

Try to make the arrival of the newcomer a positive experience for the resident dog by paying particular attention to him when the new cat is present. In that way, Poochie will associate the cat's presence with good things for him.

Both pets should have a way to escape the attentions of the other. A baby gate is a wonderful tool, because it offers the possibility of safe interactions through the grillwork. Use the baby gate to shut off the cat's room. In most cases, the kitten can pass through the gate or the cat can jump over it, but the dog is barred entrance. Therefore, Kitty is able to regulate interaction and escape into the room when necessary.

CAT MEETS NEW CANINE

In most cases, a confident resident cat will accept a new puppy quite easily. When the resident cat is healthy, she can stay out of the overeager puppy's way and quickly teach him his place with a few well-aimed swats. The pack-oriented puppy tends to readily accept Kitty's rule as the dominant fur-person in residence.

It's more difficult for an adult cat to accept an adult dog, however. In these instances, it's very important that the dog have at least rudimentary obedience training. Cats that have had previous positive experiences with dogs adapt more readily than those that have never before experienced canine company.

The same principles apply when you introduce the dog to the cat or kitten, but in this case, it's the new canine that will be placed in a segregated area. Kitty should already be familiar with the smell of the dog from the planted scented object. Have a friend bring Poochie to your house in a crate or on a leash. If the cat is interested, let her check out the newcomer immediately. Cats that hide should be left alone; put Poochie in his room, and let the two become acquainted beneath the door at their own pace. It's important that the cat retain her run of the house and control of as much of her territory as possible. The cat's routine should be disturbed as little as possible.

When Kitty is interested, let her approach the puppy at her own speed. Place the dog in a crate or on a leash. Shy cats may ignore the interloper, while confident cats may walk right up to the canine for a face-to-face encounter. Try using the baby gate to encourage introductions at the cat's pace.

Making everybody smell the same is a trick that helps cats accept strange animals into the house. Cats identify approved items and family members by rubbing against them to spread their own familiar scent. Rub brewer's yeast into the fur of both pets to help the new dog smell similar to the resident cat. This may help ease introductions.

Treat the encounter as business as usual. Get a cup of coffee, read a magazine, turn on the TV. It's very likely that Kitty will throw a fit, hiss, spit, and growl at the dog, but this is normal feline etiquette. Unless the cat actually tries to hurt a tiny puppy, let her get it out of her system. She'll feel much better. If the cat tries to attack the dog or gets too rough with the puppy, say "No!" and use your squirt bottle to interrupt the behavior, then remove the new pet, and try again later.

Again, each pet should have a private safe place to escape from the other one. For the dog, this will at first be the segregated room, and eventually his private crate. Kitty should be able to stay above dangerous dog-level by lounging on chairbacks, tabletops, and windowsills.

INTRODUCING SHY PETS AND CONFIDENT PETS

Matching a dominant resident to a fearful arrival usually works well, because the dominant pet takes charge of the situation. As long as no aggression develops between them, the shy newcomer will soon learn there's nothing to fear.

But introducing a dominant, in-your-face newcomer to a fearful or insecure resident pet will take much patience and self-control on your part. Fearful pets do best with gentle and controlled introductions in pleasant circumstances, with an enjoyable distraction going on at the same time. Pet your insecure old-timer, or engage him with a treat or toy. Feeding them both at the same time but at opposite ends of the same room often works well, as the pets are aware of each other but have something more important to occupy them.

Most anxious pets do quite well in familiar surroundings. Once you get Shrinking Violet over the hump of introductions so that she knows there's nothing to fear, the relationship generally moves along swimmingly. Keep in mind, however, that a dominant newcomer may bully a shy resident pet in order to establish social status. That may seem unfair and even cruel to you when your beloved Shrinking Violet is pestered in her own home. Control yourself, though, and let the two work out their differences themselves. Championing the underdog or -cat and preventing a definitive victory from occurring will only postpone the inevitable. As long as the two pets aren't able to decide who is boss, the bullying behavior will go on and on and on. Don't interfere, but do support the status of the dominant pet. Once Bully Pet doesn't feel the need to prove himself, the tension should ease and Shrinking Violet will find her new place in the scheme of things and enjoy her life again.

When your resident pet is a nervous, fearful cat, the new dog doesn't have to be particularly dominant to cause problems. Just the change in the status quo may be enough to cause behavior problems in the resident cat. Cats who have never before experienced dogs may simply hide. In the most serious instances, Kitty becomes an invisible presence in her own house. She may lose her appetite, groom herself bald, or wet outside the litter box.

DEFUSING AGGRESSION

Dogs and cats most commonly act aggressive toward each other when their territory and/or their social status is challenged. Aggression is also generated by competition over food, toys, prime resting places, and owner attention. It can arise either because they are dominant individuals or because they are fearful and become defensive.

It's been said before but bears repeating: the best way to reduce aggression in pets is to have them neutered. Abstinence can leave a sexually intact pet edgy, something a cold shower won't fix.

Sharing your bed with a furry cat or dog may be pleasant on cold winter mornings, but it can send the wrong message to an aggressive pet. Sleeping in close proximity to the leader (you) confers status on the pet, and he may consider himself your social equal. Banishing both pets from your bed—not from your bedroom, they can sleep on the floor—will send an unmistakable message about who's in charge.

Also, examine the aggressive pet's diet. Cut out table snacks, and feed only high-quality commercial food. We tend to feed our pets the equivalent of rocket fuel and then wonder why they tear around the house. All that energy has to go somewhere, and is better spent chasing a ball or a fishing-pole toy than chasing the other pet. Most dogs require at least thirty minutes of aerobic exercise every day, and cats benefit greatly from regular exercise as well.

Make sure there is enough territory to go around. Adding vertical space like elevated perches to satisfy the cat will go a

long way toward soothing ruffled fur, since second-story territory won't be in dispute.

Also ensure there are enough toys to go around. Two or
three will not be sufficient; offer them a dozen each. The toys
should be rotated, not left out at all times for you to trip over.
Pets tend to become bored when offered the same toys every day.

Reserve each pet's favorite toy for use as a reward during
training, but have another favorite available at all times, prefer-
ably something that is dog- or cat-specific. A nylon chew bone
for the dog is good, because it's generally too heavy for Kitty to
swipe. Something like a Cat Track toy may be the ticket for the
cat, but a Ping-Pong ball inside a cat carrier, or a wad of alu-
minum foil inside an empty tissue box, is a cheaper alternative.

In addition to these favorites, offer a couple of different toys
to the dog and cat each day, perhaps a Frisbee for the dog or a
catnip mouse for Kitty. Have the aggressive pet "earn" his interactive play sessions. He must "sit" before you'll engage in a
game of fetch or bring out the fishing-pole cat tease. Rotate the
toys regularly, so the pets won't become bored.

Structure the interaction so that your pets are not in competition for your attention. Play with the cat while Poochie is
outdoors taking care of his business; play with Poochie during
one of Kitty's interminable naps.

BUILDING CONFIDENCE

Many of the same techniques for tempering aggression will help
build confidence in the shy pet. The proper diet and the provi-
sion of an adequate amount of space will work wonders. In addition, obedience training and play therapy are very effective tools.

Obedience training in both cats and dogs will build confidence because you are giving the pet a chance to excel and be
praised. In *shy dogs only,* games of tug-of-war will build confidence. Use an old towel or sock, and allow the dog to win by
eventually releasing your end; praise the dog for his victory. *But
never play tug-of-war with an aggressive or dominant dog;* it
could cause the aggression to escalate.

For cats, predatory games of chase-and-catch are particularly helpful. Use a fishing-pole toy to engage the cat in a game

of stalk-and-pounce. Allow the cat to win by catching the tro-
phy. Praise Kitty for her assertiveness.

CANINE "ACCIDENTS"

House-training is a fact of life for the indoor dog, but even a dog
who knows better will leave an unwelcome deposit from time to
time. Some accidents are due to a health problem, while others
are prompted by stress brought on by the arrival of a new pet.

Leg-lifting in the house is a display of dominance that can
be drastically curtailed by having the dog neutered. By defecating on the owner's bed, shoes, or other belongings, Poochie
makes the object more his own by sharing his scent. Both dominant and insecure dogs leave these presents as a kind of wake-
up call telling owners they're in distress. Refer to the previous
section for ways to curb aggression or overcome shyness.

The adult dog may need a refresher course in house-training,
and puppies definitely need guidance. It's actually easy to house-
break dogs because of their built-in attitude toward cleanliness.
Dogs avoid messing their bed, so during house-training, the dog
should be confined to a space only large enough for bedding and
a small bowl of water. He'll do his best to wait until you take
him outside, so he doesn't have to sleep with his waste. That's
why the small bathroom or laundry room rarely works for
house-training. Poochie simply sleeps at one end of the room and
uses the other end as his toilet.

Confinement in a *small* place—a plain cardboard box or
dog crate—is best. Then you must anticipate his internal clock
by providing regular breaks. Feed him at the same time every day
so you can predict when he needs to go, and take him to the
same place so he'll recognize the scent and area as his "potty
place." To avoid accidents on the way from the crate to the door,
carry the dog if he's small enough, or put him on a leash so he's
under your command. Dogs are less likely to eliminate when
they're working.

Until he's reliable, the dog should be confined whenever he
is not under your direct supervision. That way, if a mistake does
happen, he'll be caught in the act—that's the *only* time corrections will have any effect.

Tell him "no" in mid-squat, and immediately remove him to the designated area. Link a command to the action, and praise him when he finishes doing his business in the right place. As he squats, tell him, "Hurry up, hurry up," and then praise him when he's done. Eventually he'll know what's expected when he hears you say, "Hurry up." It is helpful to leave his last deposit in the area so the scent will remind him what he's there to do. (This may not be possible for apartment dwellers.)

Reprimands after the fact *do not work*. If you've left the dog unsupervised—to answer the phone, let's say, or to watch TV—and you then find his deposit under the piano, all you can do is clean it up and resolve to watch him closer next time. Eliminate opportunities for mistakes by confining him when he cannot be watched. He'll soon learn to let someone know when he needs to go out, in order to avoid messing his bed.

Most puppies learn the concept within the first several days, and even headstrong adults can be house-trained within two or three weeks with consistent confinement. However, puppies may be physically incapable of reliable control until they're six months old. That doesn't mean you need to box Puppy for the whole time; he'll improve all along the way and should learn to notify you of his needs whether he's confined or not.

Pet doors are a wonderful invention, and allow pets to come and go into their confined yard at their own whim so you don't have to play doorman. If your cat is not allowed outdoors but Poochie needs easy access to his outdoor toilet, there are pet doors available (Staywell Security Doors) that require a "key" to open. Only pets with the special collar can open the door. That keeps Kitty in but lets Poochie out, and also prevents wildlife from following a pet inside.

LITTER PROBLEMS

The mother cat usually teaches her kittens how to use the litter box. However, cats may miss or refuse to use the box for health reasons or to communicate stress. Because cats thrive on the status quo, the arrival of a new pet often results in stress.

Spraying is the equivalent of canine leg-lifting; having the cat neutered will reduce or even eliminate the behavior. Like

dogs, cats may wet or leave deposits on owner-identified territory as a way of spreading a familiar, comforting scent. Review
the earlier section on building your pet's confidence, and be sure
to take your time performing introductions to help smooth the
transition.

Other important factors also contribute to elimination problems. Unlike dogs, cats may not accept your choice of potty location. The litter box must be convenient to use but in a relatively
private location. It must not be so close to the cat's food or sleeping quarters as to offend feline sensibilities, and it absolutely
must be clean or the cat may refuse to use it. Don't expect cats
to share; provide one litter box for each cat.

Some dogs, particularly terrier breeds, like to dig in the cat's
litter box, and most dogs seem to enjoy eating the contents
(ugh!). This behavior is enough to prompt many cats to find
alternative bathroom facilities. If you see this happening, choose
a covered litter box with an opening that is too small to accommodate the dog. Another option is to put the litter box on a table
beyond Poochie's reach; most cats can access these high areas.

A more elaborate solution is to place the litter box in a
closet, laundry room, or enclosed porch and then install a baby
gate or pet door that Poochie can't breach. Or try looping a rope
around the doorknob and anchoring it so that the door opens
far enough for Kitty to come and go but does not allow the dog
to pass.

CANINE CHEWING

Those who've always lived with cats may be amazed at the damage a dog can do with his teeth. Puppies are notorious chewers
while teething, as are kittens, but most dogs never outgrow the
chewing urge. They use chewing to relieve boredom.

Shoes are a favorite with dogs, because they not only feel
good (all that leather!) but carry the scent of Poochie's beloved
owner. Chewing your shoes makes him feel closer to you.

Offer Poochie appropriate chew toys to keep him from
gnawing the table legs. Real bones are out; they're unsanitary,
and they're dangerous because they splinter and can cause life-
threatening intestinal blockage or perforation when swallowed.

Rawhide chews are a favorite with dogs, but don't overdo them. Big dogs don't just chew, they eat the things; too much swallowed rawhide can interfere with digestion and cause constipation or even blockage.

The best chew toys for dogs are the Nylabone or Gumabone products. They're available at most pet supply stores, and come in a variety of sizes and flavors for every dog's taste. When you catch Poochie chewing a forbidden item, say "no" and give him the alternative.

SCRATCHING ETIQUETTE

Cats don't chew furniture, but they do scratch it. Claw marks are also a way to mark territory, and scratching can be a sign of dominance in the cat.

As with the chewing dog, you need to offer the scratching cat a better alternative. Each cat has her own taste in scratching surfaces, whether horizontal or vertical, soft or hard; take a cue from her choice of inappropriate targets. If she scratches the hardwood floor, provide a hard horizontal surface. Offer her a fabric-covered vertical post if she likes to claw the back of the sofa, or give her a piece of carpet if the rug is her choice. The object should be tall enough or long enough to accommodate the cat's full-length stretch, and stable enough so it won't tip over under feline assault.

As with the litter box, location is the key to getting the cat to use a commercial post. Since scratching is a way to mark territory, don't expect Kitty to hide her habit in a back room. Cats enjoy a good scratch after eating, so placing the post near the food bowl is a good choice. A conspicuous location will draw the cat's attention and encourage continued use of the post.

Wean her from scratching unacceptable objects by placing the commercial post directly in front of the old, inappropriate target, like the sofa. Use your squirt bottle to dissuade her each time she scratches the wrong item, and praise her for using the correct one. Draw her attention to it by luring her with a feather or string dangled against the surface. When she grabs for the toy, praise her as she sinks claws into the post. Spiking the post with catnip may also help. Once she starts making the correct scratching choice, you can gradually move the commercial post away from the sofa to a more permanent position, if you wish.

SUPPERTIME BLUES

Feeding pets in the interspecies family can be problematic, particularly if Poochie is a gorger and Kitty's a nibbler. The dog stays healthier when meal fed, but will still eat the cat kibble if you've left it out all day for Kitty. It is unhealthy for dogs and cats to eat each other's food, and pets are quite possessive about their food and may become defensive or even aggressive if another pet trespasses.

The easiest way to feed cats and dogs together is to give them their meals at the same time at opposite ends of the kitchen, but in some cases, separate rooms may be necessary.

It is possible to free-feed the cat while meal-feeding the canine gorger. When the cat is an athlete able to navigate the heights, place the cat food bowl on a table the dog can't reach.

Another option is to place the cat's bowl in a room blocked off with a pet gate that Kitty can vault but that the dog cannot negotiate. Or feed the cat inside a carrier or cage that's too small for the dog to enter. Kitty can come and go at will, and nibble throughout the day, and her kibble will remain safe from the dog.

If you have a bruiser of a cat who's having his way with the dog's food, reverse some of the same techniques to protect the canine turf. Usually, you'll simply have to meal-feed the dog, and ensure Poochie's privacy until he's finished.

IN CLOSING

Most problems between dogs and cats in the home are matters of misunderstanding. People who have always had cats may not realize what's involved when a dog enters the equation, and vice versa. By understanding the basic differences and similarities between your pets, you'll be better prepared to deal with care and behavior issues that may arise.

Successful introductions may take a few hours to a couple of weeks, depending on the individual cat and dog. But with the right preparation and lots of patience and understanding, you can help the new kid in town become a welcome member of your existing pet family.

Com*pet*ability is not only possible, it is uniquely rewarding. Dogs and cats build lasting relationships with each other. They play together and sleep together and become a part of each other's family. You *can* build your own peaceable kingdom with dogs and cats, and you'll reap the rewards for years to come.

Further Reading

MAGAZINES

CATS Magazine
Box 1790
Peoria, IL 61656

Cat Fancy
Box 6050
Mission Viejo, CA 92690

I Love Cats
950 Third Avenue, 16th Floor
New York, NY 10022

Dog Fancy
Box 6050
Mission Viejo, CA 92690

Dog World Magazine
29 North Wacker Drive
Chicago, IL 60606

PetLife
1227 West Magnolia Avenue
Fort Worth, TX 76104

CARE BOOKS

Carlson, Delbert, and James Giffen. *Cat Owner's Home Veterinary Handbook*. New York: Howell Book House, 1995.

Carlson, Delbert, and James Giffen. *Dog Owner's Home Veterinary Handbook*. New York: Howell Book House, 1992.

Shojai, Amy D. *The Purina Encyclopedia of Cat Care*. New York: Ballantine, 1998.

Siegal, Mordecai, ed. *The Cornell Book of Cats*. New York: Villard, 1989.

Siegal, Mordecai, ed. *U.C. Davis Book of Dogs*. New York: HarperCollins, 1995.

BEHAVIOR AND TRAINING BOOKS

Dodman, Nicholas. *The Dog Who Loved Too Much*. New York: Bantam, 1996.

Shojai, Amy D. *Kitten Care and Training*. New York: Howell Book House, 1996.

Whiteley, Ellen H. *Understanding and Training Your Cat or Kitten*. New York: Crown Publishers, 1994.

Whiteley, Ellen H. *Understanding and Training Your Dog or Puppy*. New York: Crown Publishers, 1995.

Wright, John C., and Judi Wright Lashnits. *Is Your Cat Crazy?* New York: Macmillan, 1994.

Resources

American Humane Association
Animal Protection Division
63 Inverness Drive East
Englewood, CO 80112
(animal welfare)

American Society for the
Prevention of Cruelty to
Animals
424 East 92nd Street
New York, NY 10128
(animal welfare)

American Veterinary Society of
Animal Behavior
Wayne Hunthausen, President
Westwood Animal Hospital
4820 Rainbow Boulevard
Westwood, KS 66205

Animal Behavior Associates
Suzanne Hetts and Daniel Q. Estep
4994 South Independence Way
Littleton, CO 80123
(certified applied animal behavior
society)

Animal Behavior Society
John C. Wright, Chair
Board of Professional Certification
Psychology Department
Mercer University
Macon, GA 31207
(society of animal behaviorists)

Association of Pet Dog Trainers
Box 385
Davis, CA 95617
1-800-PET-DOGS

Delta Society
Box 1080
Renton, WA 98057-9906
(human-animal interaction)

Friends of Animals
777 Post Road, Suite 205
Darien, CT 06820
(low-cost neutering)

Appendixes

1. DANGER SIGNALS IN CATS AND DOGS

SIGNS OF HEALTH PROBLEMS

ANY CHANGE IN ELIMINATION HABITS:

Increased bowel movements

Decreased bowel movements

Diarrhea

Constipation

Increased urination

Decreased urination

A break in litter box or house-training

Blood in the feces or urine

ANY CHANGE IN EATING HABITS:

Loss of appetite or refusal to eat

Increased thirst

Voracious appetite without weight gain

Fluctuation in weight—gain or loss

Vomiting, especially blood in vomit

Abnormal discharge from eyes, ears, or nose

CHANGE IN BREATHING:

Coughing, wheezing, sneezing, difficulty breathing

CHANGE IN SKIN:

Excessive scratching or licking

Scabby or sore skin

Fur thinning or loss with bald patches

Lump or bump anywhere on body

OVERT SIGNS:

Bleeding

Loss of consciousness

Limping

Soliciting attention with vocalizations (whines, meows, etc.)

SUBTLE SIGNS:

Hiding and avoiding contact

Refusing to move

2. CAT AND DOG LIFE SIGNS

SPECIES	*TEMPERATURE	†PULSE AT REST	RESPIRATION AT REST
NEONATAL KITTEN	96–100°F	200–300 beats per minute	25–45 breaths per minute
ADULT CAT	100.5–102.5°F	160–240 beats per minute	20–30 breaths per minute
NEONATAL PUPPY	96–100°F	220 beats per minute	25–45 breaths per minute
ADULT DOG	100–102.5°F	‡60–150 beats per minute, up to 180 in toy breeds	10–30 breaths per minute

*Measure using a rectal thermometer.

†Place fingers at juncture of inside thigh and body, or over left elbow above heart to feel pulse.

‡Larger dogs have comparatively slower rates than small dogs.

3. VACCINATION SCHEDULE*

AGE OF PET	DOG VACCINATION	CAT VACCINATION
6 TO 8 WEEKS	canine distemper, measles, parainfluenza (CPI), and parvovirus	panleukopenia (FPV), rhinotracheitis (FVR), and calicivirus (FCV)
8 TO 12 WEEKS	DHLPP (distemper, hepatitis, leptospirosis, parainfluenza, parvovirus) and sometimes coronavirus	second FPV, FVR, and FCV; if recommended by vet, test for FeLV and vaccinate if negative
16 WEEKS	rabies and second DHLPP	rabies, third FPV, FVR, and FCV; second FeLV if recommended
12 MONTHS AND ANNUALLY THEREAFTER	rabies† and DHLPP with or without coronavirus, as recommended	rabies† and FPV, FVR, and FCV with or without FeLV, as recommended

*The age of the pet and the incidence of the disease in a given region will influence what protection is necessary; always follow your veterinarian's recommendation.

†One-year and three-year rabies vaccinations are available; protocol varies from state to state.

4. COMPARING ILLNESSES COMMON TO DOGS AND CATS

CONDITION	CAT SIGNS	DOG SIGNS	CAT TREATMENT	DOG TREATMENT
ALLERGY, FLEA	rear half itching, miliary dermatitis	rear half itching	flea treatment	flea treatment
ALLERGY, ATOPY	miliary dermatitis	front half itching and ear infections	avoid allergen, sometimes allergy shots	avoid allergen, sometimes allergy shots
ALLERGY, FOOD	face, mouth, and ear itchiness	itchiness all over	diagnosis with elimination diet and avoid eating allergen	diagnosis with elimination diet and avoid eating allergen
ARTHRITIS	refusal to move	limping, difficulty getting up	massage, warm compresses, staying slim	massage, warm compresses, staying slim, aspirin
DENTAL DISEASE	crusty buildup at gum line, bleeding gums, bad breath, receding gums, decay	yellow to brown buildup at gum line, bleeding gums, bad breath, broken teeth	veterinary dentistry, home dental care	veterinary dentistry, home dental care
COCCIDIOSIS*	loose stool with mucus and blood	same as in cats	sulfa-type drug	same as in cats
GIARDIASIS*	similar to signs of coccidiosis	same as in cats	metronidazole	same as in cats
HOOKWORMS*	rare in cats	bloody, deep red, or tarlike stool	pyrantel pamoate	same as in cats
ROUNDWORMS*	potbelly, dull fur, diarrhea or mucus in stool, spaghetti-type worms in stool	same as in cats	pyrantel pamoate	same as in cats
TAPEWORMS*	ricelike segments caught in fur near tail or in stool	same as in cats	Droncit pills or injection; flea eradication	same as in cats
WHIPWORMS*	rare in cats	diarrhea, anemia, weight loss	veterinary treatment; keeping stools picked up	same as in cats

*Intestinal parasites

Disease	Signs in Cats	Treatment in Cats	Signs in Dogs	Treatment in Dogs
CUTEREBRA†	most common in cats; swelling on neck or chest	surgical removal by veterinarian; limit hunting	less common in dogs, same signs as in cats	same as in cats
TICKS†	uncommon in cats; usually between toes or on back of neck	remove with tweezers; prevent by using approved insecticides	common in dogs; often inside or around ears	same as in cats
BABESIOSIS‡	does not affect cats	not applicable	high fever, weakness, loss of appetite, bloody urine, incoordination, teeth grinding	antiprotozoal medications from veterinarian; prevent by removing ticks within 12 to 24 hours of attachment and use approved insecticide
CYTAUXZOONOSIS‡	loss of appetite, depression, high fever, anemia, dehydration, sometimes jaundice	no treatment; prevent by removing ticks within 12 to 24 hours of attachment and by keeping cats indoors; use approved insecticide	does not affect dogs	not applicable
EHRLICHIOSIS‡	does not affect cats	not applicable	fever, loss of appetite, eye and nasal discharge, swollen legs, nosebleeds	tetracycline; prevent by removing ticks within 12 to 24 hours of attachment, and use approved insecticide
TICK PARALYSIS‡	does not affect cats	not applicable	incoordination or weakness of hind legs, progressive paralysis	removal of ticks
LYME DISEASE‡	no known signs	not applicable	sudden lameness	antibiotics, remove ticks within 12 to 24 hours of attachment, use approved insecticide, vaccination sometimes recommended
ROCKY MOUNTAIN‡ SPOTTED FEVER	does not affect cats	not applicable	fever, loss of appetite, arthritis signs, coughing or labored breathing, hunching, swelling of face or extremities	tetracycline, prevent by removing ticks within 12 to 24 hours, and use approved insecticide
EAR MITES†	head shaking, dark crumbly exudate inside ears, scratching at ears	clean ears, apply approved insecticide, sometimes ivermectin injection	same as in cats	same as in cats

†External parasites
‡Tick-borne diseases

4. COMPARING ILLNESSES COMMON TO DOGS AND CATS (cont.)

CONDITION	CAT SIGNS	DOG SIGNS	CAT TREATMENT	DOG TREATMENT
RINGWORM	bald patches; especially affects kittens and immune-compromised cats	bald patches; especially affects puppies and immune-compromised dogs	self-cure in 60 to 100 days; oral medicine (griseofulvin) and/or lime dip, sometimes vaccination	same as in cats
DIABETES	eating and drinking a lot, excessive urination, missing the litter box	eating and drinking a lot, excessive urination, accidents in house	reduce overweight, sometimes oral medication but usually insulin injections	reduce overweight, usually insulin injections
HEART DISEASE	labored breathing, weakness or fainting spells, edema, sudden hind limb pain or paralysis; no coughing	harsh dry cough usually at night or after exercise, labored breathing, weakness, fainting, edema	veterinary-prescribed medication, sometimes taurine supplement; cats rarely survive more than a few months	veterinary-prescribed medication to control problems over the long term, even years
HEARTWORM DISEASE	breathing problems as in asthma; collapse, coughing, vomiting	coughing, shortness of breath, fainting after exercise, labored breathing, edema	none; preventative medication available	thiacetarsamide injections, enforced rest, further medication to kill microfilaria; preventative medication available
KIDNEY DISEASE	increased thirst and urination, missing litter box, loss of appetite, losing weight, vomiting, diarrhea or constipation, mouth sores, ammonia breath	same as in cats	veterinary medication, prescription diet	same as in cats
LOWER URINARY TRACT DISEASE	break in house-training, dribbling urine, bloody urine, straining without result, crying during urination	same as in cats; also splay-legged posture during urination or splattery stream	dietary intervention, catheterization	same as in cats; also antibiotic therapy, sometimes surgery
RABIES	vicious, violent actions, spooky eyes, increased vocalization, wobbly gait	same as in cats; also often jaw paralysis with drooling	no treatment; vaccinate to prevent	no treatment; vaccinate to prevent

5. CANCER: WHAT TO LOOK FOR

CANCER SIGNS IN PETS*

Swellings that persist or continue to grow

Sores that don't heal

Weight loss

Appetite loss

Bleeding or other discharge

Bad odor

Difficulty eating

Exercise intolerance

Ongoing lameness or stiffness

Difficulty breathing or eliminating

Source: Veterinary Cancer Society

Index